Permission to Rage

The Book on How to Complain Effectively

Edward Field

With letters by Ahmed Dahl

LightMouse

First published in Great Britain in 2014 by LightMouse.

www.LightMouse.co.uk

Illustrations © Edward Field 2014

All illustrations by Genesis Rodrigues. Twitter: genesisfrr

Cover design by The Dream Loft – www.thedreamloft.co.uk

ISBN 13: 978-0-9930583-0-1

ISBN 10: 0-9930583-0-2

Also by the Author

**As Eebee Field, contributing children's playwright,
published by Via Afrika Publishers:**

Afrikaans Huistal Graad 7 Leesboek – Elartie en die Ergbert (Elarty and the Ergbert)
Afrikaans Huistal Graad 8 Leesboek – So Sê Mens (So Says Human)

Afrikaans Huistal Graad 9 Leesboek – Sjokolade (Chocolate)

As editor, published by The Dream Loft:

The Haunting of Tyler May by B. J. Mears
The Thieves of Antiquity by B. J. Mears
The Brimstone Chasm by B. J. Mears
Gallows Iron by B. J. Mears

As The Squiss:

Film reviews, fiction, inspiration rants and cake at **www.squiss.co.uk**

For Marieke, with few complaints and none with validity.

Special thanks to:
Lesley Bootiman, author, inspiration, support, gift from The Princes Trust and friend; Shosh Copley, for the idea for this book and for the enjoyable exchange of rants; Bag, for his contribution of complaints; Matt Sims, for permission to complain on his behalf; Genesis Rodrigues for her illustrations; Danilo Rodrigues for illustration assistance; Ahmed Dahl, for permitting me to publish a few of his fantastic letters; Mark Porthouse for technical trickery; Angela Merriott for proofreading; and finally, but perhaps predominantly, Ben Mears for the donkey work in all technical matters required for putting my work on the page, both paper and digital.

Contents

Chapters

Chapter 1: A History of Complaints - Mine & Theirs

Lesson 1

My first complaint, that I recall, was one Saturday evening at home in the back end of the '70s. Margaret Thatcher had yet to rise and, on reflection, one might be excused for imagining it to be the dark ages.

Dad was probably out decorating somebody's house in return for a frozen chicken and my siblings and I were seated around the Formica counter that rested on the Hotpoint Twin Tub and doubled as our kitchen table. Our mother was busy cremating the Findus Crispy Pancakes, mashing green potatoes, boiling the life out of the cabbage and generally crumpling under the weight of poverty, four children and an era before the 'new man' had been invented.

It was probably the fault of *The Dukes of Hazzard*. The cause has faded from my mind; the consequences indelibly marked upon it. The General Lee was mere minutes away from launching itself into the air, only to land at an inexplicable angle with nary a dent or scratch, and dinner was taking too damn long.

I began to hum.

The tune, familiar to all as a Christmas carol, had alternative lyrics equally familiar to parents and children alike. My siblings smirked and my mother spun around, lumpy mash hurtling across the tiny kitchen and thudding on the faux-cork tiles, challenging me, knowingly, through gritted teeth.

"Why are you singing *O Come, All Ye Faithful* in the middle of June?"

"I'm not. I'm humming *Why Are We Waiting?*"

I learned four lessons in the moments that followed:

1. Potato mashers hurt.

2. Very occasionally, honesty is absolutely *not* the best policy.

3. Nights are longer with an empty belly.

4. Choose your complaints and the manner in which you complain *very* carefully.

*

Lesson 2

Fast-forward ten years and, though I had just left home, I had so far failed to escape the dead-end town. I had embarked upon my first serious, disastrous relationship, was making plans, dreaming big and working full time as a glorified shelf stacker at Medicare. My short hair was reaching towards my collar, my tattoo taunted the world rebelliously beneath my clothing and my boldest statement, a discreet, antique gold ring, stuck a middle finger up at my tiny, conservative world from my left ear.

I felt confident, I looked good and I was beginning to find my place.

Then the area manager visited the store, took one look at me and proclaimed to my manager, "Only two types of men have earrings: Thugs and poofs! Tell him to take it out or find another job."

It begged the question, *Which am I? Thug or poof?* In the ultra-conservative backwater where I lived, neither label thrilled me. The biggest trouble I'd been in was a detention for talking in a maths class, and I couldn't fathom why someone's sexuality should be an insult.

At that time the only member of staff at Medicare who didn't have at least one ear pierced was the manager, a former Marine who wouldn't have been seen dead with jewelry adorning his body, beyond his wedding band, but didn't give two hoots what I put on or through mine. The remaining five members of staff, all women, each wore earrings ranging from dainty diamond studs to wind chimes that dangled below their chins. Long before it became popular, I heralded it as a distinct case of 'gender discrimination' and vowed to take the area manager on.

My manager groaned and suggested I remove the earring during working hours and let it go in favour of a peaceful life, but I spotted an opportunity for good to triumph over evil and for David to put one squarely in the centre of Goliath's forehead.

Even back then, I knew I needed two things: Evidence and a case to answer. Evidence was easy; the manager couldn't deny it had occurred. As for the case, I referred to the Medicare bible. Naturally there was nothing stating it was company policy that men may not wear earrings. The only mention of jewelry I could find was in the health and safety manual where a short paragraph stated that jewelry must not hinder work or represent a danger to the wearer or other person. No mention of gender. Bingo!

Unless I crawled across the floor or wiped the left side of my face along the goods cages, there was little chance of the ring catching on anything and, if The Powers That Be decided it *was* a danger and demanded its removal, they would have to enforce it across the board.

Smelling victory and a triumph for justice and the underdog I wrote two virtually identical letters: one to the regional manager and another to my local MP, a certain Lib Dem politician who was the champion of our community and making serious waves in Parliament. His name? Paddy Ashdown.

A few days later I received my first letter from the House of Commons. Mr. Ashdown wrote that he was appalled at the blatant discrimination shown to me by the area manager and that his stance was clearly unfair and illegal but, unfortunately, as I was a part-time employee and had worked for Medicare for under four years, I had no employment rights as such and so, essentially, Medicare could treat me as they pleased.

However, he continued, whilst he couldn't force the area manager or Medicare to back down, he was very happy to "publicly embarrass" them in Parliament.

When I returned to work, earring in place, my manager greeted me with raised eyebrows. Mr. Ashdown had also outlined his offer to the Medicare head office and word had filtered through rapidly with impressive results. Yes, my manager was miffed with me for rocking the boat (though he acknowledged his respect), the area manager was monumentally cheesed off and my card was marked but, ultimately, I kept both job and earring.

I'm not sure what Medicare took from the affair, as it was absorbed by Superdrug soon after, but I learned the benefit of having influential people on my side and that even with no 'rights' it is possible to see justice administered.

*

Lesson 3

In 1996 I returned to full time education as a mature student, training as a stage manager at the Bristol Old Vic Theatre School. In addition to the lectures and productions I also became live-in caretaker and each day had the run of the school once the last of the stragglers had departed. Beyond the fantastic opportunities for pranks and other deviant activities, I staged weekly games nights for anywhere between two and thirty staff and students.

Alas, the all-time favourite, Monopoly, was not in my games cupboard as my mother had kept the family set. A quick trip to WHSmith offered only the choice of a tacky, garish plastic 'luxury' edition or numerous themed versions, none of which matched the much-loved, wooden house/hotel version I missed. I recalled a special edition with silver houses and gold hotels had once been issued but that was clearly going to be way beyond the budget of an impoverished student so I wrote to Hasbro UK for advice on where to find an original set, bearing in mind this was long before the meteoric rise of eBay and Amazon.

My letter was ignored.

One Saturday morning, severely narked at being woken by noisy students requiring access to rehearsal studios on my day off, I vented my frustration in a letter to Hasbro. Why had they decided to ignore me? Was the satisfaction of their customers not of any interest in them? Were they too busy spending their profits to listen to the queries of their clientele? I repeated my original question but with more, ah, *emphasis*. *What on earth were they doing producing cheap, tacky, plastic crap instead of the superior quality of yesteryear's versions?* In hindsight, I may have ranted a little. Regardless, steam spurting less quickly from my ears, I sealed the envelope, plonked a second-class stamp on upside down and stomped along Pembroke Road to post it.

I thought no more of the letter until the following Saturday when I was disturbed a little after dawn again. Instead of more students, on the other side of the door stood the postman with a letter of apology from Hasbro and the conciliatory gift of a game of Monopoly. Yes, it was the tacky version but it was still a gift, it was free and it was the result of a complaint. I tried the same critical approach with Jaguar (*Dear Sir, I find your XK to be cheap and tacky...*) but to no avail. Nevertheless, it was yet another lesson that set me on a lifelong mission of complaining when a good complaint is called for.

And *that* is the crux of the matter.

*

Ask around the globe and there are characteristics for which the British are universally known: Bad teeth, queuing, traditionally poor cuisine, eccentricity and, most prominently, an absolute obsession with the weather.

Firstly, we have a complete inability to deal with it; when it rains we have floods, give us two dry weeks and we run out of water, our oldest oaks take flight in the wind, we panic (or drive like maniacs) if there's fog and give us a couple of inches of snow and the country grinds to a halt. It happens every year, it's been happening every year for millennia and yet it still takes us by surprise and every change of weather condition makes the headlines on the news bulletins.

But beyond, waaaaay beyond, our inability to deal with the weather is our incessant chatter about it. Meet a stranger or an old friend and the first sentence to tumble out of our mouths is something along the lines of "Hot enough for you?" or "Looks like rain again" or "Lovely day for ducks" or...

We never tire of it. How is that?

It's not just that weather drives our conversation. We moan about it incessantly. We are a nation of whingers, which isn't a problem in itself, but we confine ourselves to moaning endlessly, tediously about the weather, something over which we have absolutely no control!

But serve us cold, inedible food in a restaurant and when the waiter asks if everything is okay with the meal, instead of responding, "No, it bloody well isn't. Take it away and bring me something worthy of the extortionate sum you're charging me!" we'll nod meekly and avert our eyes. Maybe, if we're feeling particularly bold we might abstain from tipping and scuttle out guiltily with our heads bowed and pray silently that nobody noticed.

Push in front of us in a queue and, rather than challenge the queue jumper, we'll mutter into our beards, or perhaps into our neighbour's beard. "Outrageous. The cheek of it. No respect."

Well, I've had enough! I won't stand for poor service any more. No longer will I tolerate cold food, small portions, failed deliveries, rude salesmen, inadequate services, overcharging, substandard goods, unacceptable quality! And neither should you.

Since I learned to stand up for myself, to yell about my statutory rights and fight back against the rumbling, selfish, careless, antagonistic, demeaning, unpleasant, arrogant, inept, corrupt machine I have had penalties overturned, seen expenses refunded, been compensated for my troubles, I have earned bonus points, been awarded air miles, received coupons and vouchers, been presented with gifts, opened the post to find cheques, CDs, DVDs, books, tickets, teabags, chocolates, cereal bars, honey and I have received hampers and grovelling letters of apology.

Far more importantly (though you have no idea how much fun it is to find a courier standing at the door with a Fortnum & Mason hamper from your bank!), I have stood up for what is right. I have opened my mouth and shouted loudly. I have demanded justice and I have received it. I have proved myself to be right and the machine to be in the wrong. I have taken them on when they didn't expect it and I have won.

And now it is your turn.

I'm just a regular guy who had enough. I don't always achieve my goals; some monsters are too stubborn and too tightly bound in archaic traditions and weighed down by insurmountable bureaucracy. But I've learned and slowly I am being treated with respect (or perhaps they're just afraid of me now). But what I know, you can have. It's time for YOU to fight back and get the respect and service to which you are entitled.

This is your time. I give you full permission to rage!

Chapter 2: Pick Your Fights, Set Your Sights

You can complain about absolutely anything. That's your prerogative. Many people do but they tend not to be the kind of people I invite over for dinner. Life's too short to spend it in the company of grumpy people. But if you *do* have a valid reason to complain, if the service you've received has been unacceptable, then why should you remain silent? You have a voice, so use it whether you do so by phone, email, letter or in person.

I complain only when I am certain I am not in the wrong (either legally, ethically or morally). Trust me, if you start firing off complaints to people when there is no case to answer you'll be treated accordingly. It is important that there is a satisfactory reason for your complaint and it is imperative that you have your facts in order.

In 2013 I was working as a relief front of house manager at the Tobacco Factory Theatre in Bristol. It had been a long, arduous, sweaty shift, the audience had misbehaved horrendously, my staff had understandably reacted badly, the tills were out and it was the wrong side of 1 am when I finally locked the doors and headed for the car.

Parking is an unwelcome challenge in that part of Bedminster but I had squeezed my car into one of my usual spots and headed into the theatre without a second glance. Upon my return eight hours later I spied one of those evil, polythene envelopes slapped on the centre of my windscreen. I groaned inwardly, gnashed my teeth and swore vengeance on the petty gauleiter who had victimized me. *I park here all the time. There are no yellow lines and there aren't any time restrictions.*

I tore open the envelope, scanned the contents and double-checked my parking space. I had parked with my rear wheel overlapping the dropped kerb by a good six inches. A £60 fine was unwelcome, particularly after the shift I'd just endured, but if I'm happy to point the finger at injustice, I must also be prepared to admit my own failings and accept the consequences. No contest, no complaint. I paid the fine and chalked it up to experience.

However, the car park attendant in the Sainsbury's car park in Bath was a little overzealous with his sticky, polythene envelopes and I had the receipt for my baking potatoes to prove justification for parking there. So, game on. And, yes, they backed down instantly.

So what gives you the right to complain? When should you suck it up and when should you rage? I believe common sense should prevail; you know, that notion we once relied upon before we turned all litigious on each other. I'm no lawyer, I'm not dishing out legal advice here and I loathe the attitude that a lawsuit is hiding around every corner and every accident has a gold-plated lining. If you trip over an uneven paving stone it's probably because you haven't learned to walk properly or you failed to look where you were going. If, however, you fall down a dirty great hole in the middle of the pavement one night and break your leg because the council failed to put lights and barriers around it, you have every justification in seeking compensation. In which case go to a solicitor. That's not a matter for a complaint; that's a court case.

I frequently see posts on Facebook from people whingeing about the new layouts, changes to the messaging options, privacy invasions etc. I don't particularly like Facebook either. I don't understand the need to live one's private life in public; the desire to give away personal photos of one's children and tender moments for all to oogle; the compulsion to tell 1.23 billion (monthly) users that you wish your spouse a happy anniversary; or the obsession with posting photos of the food you are about to eat when it will be given back to the world in a few hours anyway. However, Facebook is an incredibly useful tool that offers massive benefits and I willingly utilize it cautiously.

So before you decide to make an official complaint to Mark Zuckerberg and his minions, there are two very simple points you need to get your head around:

1. Facebook and most other social networking sites are free. You pay nothing to use them for as long and as often as you like. Zero. Zilch. Nada. If you are receiving a service or product free of charge, providing it doesn't harm you physically or break the law, you have

very little reason to complain. Vast sprawling conglomerates frequently have little interest in ethics and they sure as hell don't feel obliged to adhere to your moral guide. If they aren't breaking the law, they can operate their service pretty much as they choose. Deal with it.

2. If you are receiving something free of charge, **YOU** are the product! Facebook is worth $150 billion (give or take a couple of billion) because of how it uses *you*.

In both cases, with Facebook and other social networking sites, **YOU** have the ultimate power here: If you don't like it, stop using it. If you want to take advantage of their sprawling, world-uniting, free service, suck it up.

Don't complain because you scalded your tongue on your latte. Coffee is supposed to be hot and you should have blown on it or waited. A letter of complaint is not justified if you watch your poodle explode when you try drying him in the microwave oven. If you're that person, complain to *me* about it in full detail because you deserve to be laughed at and I'll happily oblige.

Complaints are for rude staff, for when the frock you just bought falls apart in the first wash, for when the hotel you booked with your life savings turns out not to be the idyllic palace in the brochure but a rat-infested building site. If your statutory rights have been contravened, if the product or service you bought does not match the description, if you feel very strongly that you have been treated improperly, if external forces adversely affected your experience, *then* you are justified in your complaint. Heck, you are morally obliged to complain! Seize the day (by the throat)! As the Fraggles sang, *Catch a tail by the tiger, take the horns by the bull*. Take 'em on!

You'll need to know what your rights are, of course. We bandy about the term 'statutory rights' frequently but how many of us know exactly what they are? There is another entire book on statutory rights but I'm sure it has been written a thousand times already. My first source for advice is always the **Money Saving Expert**, Martin Lewis. If you need the information, it's almost certainly on his website, moneysavingexpert.com, and if it isn't there the site will point you in the direction of the knowledge you require. In Chapter 7, *The Complainer's Toolkit*, I have provided a list of useful resources, including Martin's site, but the essential information on statutory rights can be found at:
http://www.moneysavingexpert.com/shopping/consumer-rights-refunds-exchange.

Alternatively, just go to the website and type your query in the search box and a sprinkle of fairy dust will take you to the answer you require.

Martin uses the acronym **SAD FART**: **S**atisfactory quality, **A**s **D**escribed, **F**it for purpose **A**nd last a **R**easonable length of **T**ime. Of course, that is geared around products but, with a little imagination on your part, it works for services too.

Back in my teenage years in Chard, I was employed at a newsagents by a fine couple, Keith & Jan. They were fair, they were fun, they put up with my pranks (I spent various shifts serving customers with a paper bag over my head and took to advertising George, Jan's octogenarian father who lived above the shop, as a personal services escort, much to his merriment) and they took us all out for Christmas meals. One such meal at a grand hotel, or as grand as Chard could manage in those dark days, began with an inordinate delay during which the chef quite possibly grew everything he was serving while we starved, and continued with tepid veg, congealed gravy and slices of turkey that could best be described as *translucent*; as perfect a case of **SAD FART** you could hope to see.

We tried to eat our meals lest we upset Keith and Jan but they were having none of it. Keith took charge, complained vehemently to the restaurant manager, refused to pay a penny and marched us out en masse for pizza instead. We might have missed our traditional Christmas meal but justice was done and my memories are of a boss who stood up for his staff and took them elsewhere for a fine time.

But it isn't enough to make a valid complaint. The service is poor, you're upset, disappointment has marred your day and you've made the decision to do something about it. Excellent. Now what do you want? It's no good relying on the goodwill or intelligence of the manager you're berating to come up with a solution. Some will, but many will respond with something along the lines of "So what do you want me to do about it?"

So, what *do* you want? You have numerous options and some of them are reasonable. Some of them are written down in law (statutory rights) while many possibilities rely on generosity, goodwill and fear i.e. the fear of the perpetrator not to come across as incompetent, unethical or uncaring and, more importantly, the fear of losing your future custom and of you dissuading others from handing their cash over to them.

The first option has got to be **rectification** or **replacement**. Can they put it right or make it better right here, right now? Take our Christmas meal; the hotel manager immediately offered to reheat the meals (um, yeah, right...) and then offered to instruct the chef to start again from scratch. The apprehension of human juices infecting our replacement meals dissuaded us from accepting his offer on that occasion, but most restaurants and most people are honest, decent and hygienic and so that would be ideal. Likewise, if you notice the book you just bought has a tear across the dust jacket surely an immediate replacement is the perfect solution. It is swift, it saves time spent on letters, emails or phone calls later, and you leave with exactly what you wanted in the first place.

The second option is a **refund**. It needs no explanation and frequently you will be entitled to one. Again, at the risk of sounding repetitive, check your statutory rights first but the general rule is if the product you paid for does not do what it should, is damaged or faulty or is incorrect then you should be entitled to a full, immediate refund. For the morons and players amongst you, if you've eaten it, worn it, misused it, abused it or altered it, you're quite likely to be refused a refund and you'd better come up with a pretty good reason for doing whatever you did to it. You also need to be able to prove that a. you bought it (rather than stole it and are trying to pull a fast one) and b. you purchased it *there*. A till receipt is the most obvious proof but isn't always imperative. Asda's own-brand tinned tomatoes, for example, were clearly not bought from Waitrose. Some stores don't stock every brand in their range and may refuse a refund, in which case hotfoot it to the correct store.

Naturally, there are caveats with the whole refund option and these, too, may come down to a store's policy but, you know the drill, *check your rights first*. If you paid with cash, cash may be returned; if you paid by credit or debit card it is very likely that a refund will be made to the card and not in cash to you.

A store may offer you a credit note or gift voucher in lieu of a refund. Generally speaking, if you are not remotely at fault, you have returned the item in the condition it was sold to you and you have proved that you did indeed pay for it, you can decline the credit note in favour of the refund you deserve. However, if it is a goodwill gesture to shut you up in the face of your own incompetence, take it, thank them profusely and depart quickly before they can change their mind.

Obviously if the item was a gift, you may be faced with a challenge, particularly if Aunt Nelly sent it to you from Glasgow and you currently reside in Chelsea. Ideally Aunt Nelly will post you the receipt and everything will be peachy. However, frequently that won't be the case and so you will need to rely on the integrity and reasoning of the store manager. In December/January particularly, most of the big stores nowadays expect an influx of returned, unwanted gifts and accept the items providing they are part of their current stock and are unused, undamaged etc. Forget about a cash refund in such instances. A gift certificate or credit note is a far simpler option for you than trying to resell the item on eBay.

If the situation requires more than a quick replacement or refund, you can look at compensation. I realise I belong to a bygone era but I'm not an advocate of suing people. I don't see every little error as a reason to screw somebody out of as much money as possible, but I shall concede I like free stuff as much as the next person. If you've been put out, then why not ask for a little something extra to make up for the wasted journey, disappointment, or inconvenience? Again, it is worth knowing what you would like as a bonus just as it is imperative to outline what wrongs you expect your wrongdoer to right.

Sometimes it may be worth making a suggestion (or hinting) of what would be suitable compensation but you'll need to tread carefully with this. By all means ask for whatever you want; they can only say no. However, there is a risk of asking for too little and shooting yourself in the foot, or of asking for too much and receiving nothing. Far more importantly, if you start making monetary or material demands there is a danger of being dismissed as a gold digger rather than being viewed as a consumer with a genuine complaint.

So how do you complain? What is the process? Well, to steal a slogan, *Just do it!*

If possible, practical and likely to reap the benefits, complain immediately and at the source of the incident. If your soup is cold, ensure you didn't order gazpacho and are about to make a complete fool of yourself and then call the waiting staff over or approach the manager. If you're polite, calm and reasonable there is every chance the manager will apologise and replace it immediately. You *could* do the very British thing and apologise first ("I'm really sorry but the soup you served me is cold...") but after centuries of doing this, it's probably about time we, as a nation, grew out of this.

If you buy a new suit or frock, plonk yourself down at the local cafe to admire it and notice somebody introduced it to coffee before you got there, it is far quicker, simpler and more productive to return to the shop post-haste, point out the problem and stroll away with a replacement than it is to go home, stew about it, search for an email address, postal address or phone number and then attack the issue only to be asked to return with the item for a replacement. I know, it's common sense but you'd be amazed by the complaints I've heard and the schoolboy errors I've witnessed by people making them. Top of the list has got to be the gentleman in my Medicare days who returned a disposable razor, caked in dried shaving soap and hair, a good week or more after purchasing it and complained that it was now blunt. Let's just say the weight of his argument was somewhat diminished.

Sometimes it just isn't possible to complain at the time and source, either because the issue hasn't been noticed or, as in **Case Study 1** below, the person to whom the complaint needs to be directed isn't available. In this instance, a simple letter did the trick

Case Study 1 – Whitehall Garden Centre

This was a very simple letter of complaint. I briefly outlined my issue and stated what I expected in return.

Squircle Entertainment

Not quite a square; not quite a circle...

edward@squircleentertainment.com   www.squircleentertainment.com
Squircle Entertainment, ▓▓▓▓▓▓▓▓▓▓▓▓▓▓▓▓▓▓▓▓
+44 (0)▓▓▓▓▓▓▓   Twitter: @edwardsquircle

13 April 2014

Peter ▓▓
Whitehall Garden Centre Ltd.
Corsham Road
Lacock
Chippenham
SN15 2LZ

Dear Mr. ▓▓

My wife and I are regular patrons of your Whitchurch branch and had planned to make use of your Garden Club Days promotion for a discount on our most recent purchases. We had specifically waited until Friday 11th in order to do so, only to be informed that we had missed the promotion by a week.

I have enclosed a photocopy of the sheet we were previously given, as well as our receipt, and request that you honour the discount as, though you may have instructed that the promotion be brought forward, I am not aware that we received any notification of this and the sheet we hold states very clearly for which week it was originally arranged.

Thank you for your time and assistance in this matter and I shall look forward to hearing from you.

Yours sincerely

Edward Field.

Success rating: 5/10 – *I received what I expected a fortnight later, in the form of a letter of apology and a £5 voucher, but without bonus.*

In most cases, you have the option of a phone call, email or letter. There are advantages and drawbacks to each method and, although one method would often suffice, I would suggest in most cases a dual approach.

The advantage of complaining by phone is that you just might reach the person who has the authority to make the decision you require. Nothing beats dealing with the correct person directly, as I'll outline in Chapter 3, *Preparing for Battle*. With the right person hanging on your every word, you can explain fully, repeat the explanation if they play dim, reason with them if they become obtuse, negotiate the results and compensation you require and thank them profusely when they concede defeat. And it can all be achieved *right now* without waiting for the back and forth of written responses.

However, it can be an arduous and expensive task finding that person. Bureaucracy was invented to prevent you from getting what you deserve and telephone systems are the first line of defence for many companies. How many of us have screamed at the phone or hung up when the umpteenth menu option leads to a dead end? Help is at hand from two websites: **saynotoo870.com**, which helps find local rate alternative to the premium rate numbers money-grabbing companies would prefer you used; and **pleasepress1.com**, which gives you all the menu options so that you can press each number without having to listen to the entire menu.

Even when (or if) you reach the department you require, the chances of the manager you require being available or willing to take your call are slim and the likelihood that your message will be taken down correctly, passed along and your call returned is limited to say the least. Unless you have a direct line to the person you require, telephone complaints can be draining and, in the case of one particular villain, Utility Warehouse, may even result in a stream of verbal abuse filling your ear. But more of that in Chapter 4, *Organ Grinders & Monkeys*.

Beyond the frustration and abuse, it is essential that you have all the information to hand when making a telephone complaint. You'll need to be able to think quickly and be brave enough to deal with language issues, accents, the tribulations of call centres and, when making your follow-up calls, the frustration at never finding the same person again.

When telephone calls fail, emails and letters are your friends. Emails are quick, direct, free and, if you have set up your email correctly, you can receive a notification when your email has been opened. However, emails are notoriously disposable; they are easy to ignore; it is not always easy to find the email address of the person you require; in all likelihood your email will not be opened by the CEO but by his or her PA; many will end up in the junk folder; and sometimes gremlins in the ether swallow them. And, just in case you need another reason to be cautious, it's far too easy to hit 'send' before checking the name, address, content...

And so to the good old-fashioned letter. With the advent of email, the art of letter writing is, if not dead, then at least in a state of serious ill health. Yes, it takes longer to compose a letter than to make a phone call, it requires a stamp, you'll need to wait patiently for the letter to arrive and the reply to be received, and, unless you pay substantially more for Royal Mail's Recorded or Special

Delivery services, there is no guarantee your letter will reach its destination.

But for me, if the issue cannot be raised in person immediately, a complaint by letter wins hands down every time. Letters are far harder to ignore than emails. How many emails filled your inbox today? How many did you consign to the trash without a second thought? How many of the brown envelopes that landed on your doormat did you have the courage to shred without opening? It isn't so easy to ignore a folded sheet of paper with your name and address on it.

With a letter one can pour venom onto the page, reconsider, recompose eloquently and post with purpose. One does not accidently drop a letter into the postbox. A letter feels somehow more definite, more tangible and because it requires more effort to compose a letter than to fire off a quick email, I find they are generally taken more seriously and produce better results.

I'll go into more detail on how to prepare and compose each form of complaint in Chapter 4, *Organ Grinders & Monkeys*, but my overwhelming preference and advice is to write a fantastic letter of complaint, email a copy informing the recipient that this is to ensure at least one gets through and then, if necessary, follow up with a phone call to let them know you're serious about the matter.

In the instance of one of my recent successes, **Case Study 2** (Halfords), I initially contacted their customer service department via the online form. When I had not received a response twenty-four hours later, I sat down to write a letter to the chairman, Dennis Millard, posted it first class and followed it up immediately with an email and attached a copy of the letter:

Case Study 2 – Halfords

Requiring more detail than Case Study 1, I outlined my complaint with a far more personal slant. I needed him on my side, to identify with me and feel both sorry and obliged to rectify the problems caused to a fellow cyclist. At the very least I expected a fully functioning bike i.e. for Halfords to rectify the issues it had caused. In addition to that, I hinted at possible compensation, allowing Mr. Millard to reach his own decision following my lead: I mentioned a helmet and my need to buy secondhand shoes as seeds of thought for him to ponder, but without expectations. To ask for either outright would surely have put his back up and resulted in an instant dismissal.

Squircle Entertainment ♀
Not quite a square; not quite a circle...

edward@squircleentertainment.com   www.squircleentertainment.com   www.squiss.co.uk
Squircle Entertainment,
+44 (0)███████   Twitter: @edwardsquircle

1 July 2014

Dennis Millard, Chairman
Halfords Group plc
Icknield Street Drive
Washford West
Redditch
Worcestershire
B98 0DE

███████████████

Dear Mr Millard

On Thursday 12th June I bought an Apollo Envoy men's hybrid bike from your Eastgate branch in Bristol. It was the first new bike I have bought for about 26 years, when I was a teenager. In the intervening years I've bought cheap second hand bikes and replaced them when they have finally given up or been stolen. It's nothing to you, but for me it was a very big deal. I'd have loved to spent substantially more on a bicycle but at this stage, economically, I cannot justify it. Besides, when I raided the winemaking demijohn where I drop in all my loose change, I had sufficient to cover the £250 or so I needed to buy the bike, peddles, and (hopefully) a second hand pair of cycling shoes to fit the cleats. A new helmet and everything else will just have to wait. I know none of this matters to you, but I want to you to understand that this was a real occasion for me. The Apollo Envoy looked good, felt light, appeared to be a heck of a lot better than any bike I've ever owned, and your salesman sold its attributes convincingly.

A couple of days later, I took it out for the first time. I managed 200m before I gave up and rolled it back home. No matter what I did, most of the gears would not engage and the clicking and grinding was unbearable. After contacting your customer services, I was invited to return the bike, whereupon we discovered that the teeth were bent and a couple were actually broken or badly made (i.e. sharp and short). I was surprised that such substandard cogs were fitted to a brand new bike, but accepted the replacement and moved on.

Yesterday morning I discovered my tyre was flat. Naturally I do not blame Halfords for punctures - we all know they occur. However, the inner tube was not punctured but had split at one of the many round 'joins' on the tube. I have been working away a great deal recently, and so had managed to cycle only about 30-40 miles, so it is concerning that a brand new inner tube could split so quickly but, again, I accept that as part of cycling. However, I was a little troubled to see that the wrong size inner tube had been fitted. It is approximately 2 inches too large and was folded over twice in order to fit inside the tyre!

I duly contacted customer services again but a day later have yet to receive a response. I'm surprised that people you pay to care about the people who pay *you* don't care enough to follow up at the earliest opportunity.

Having repaired the split in the inner tube, refolded it (as a temporary measure) and re-inflated it, I took the bike out again this morning. Today the gears slipped out regularly, rather than just occasionally as I have become used to, and the pedal section (crankset?) is clicking and grinding and feels as though it is moving laterally.

I am not an experienced cyclist; ten miles at a time is my limit at the moment. It would be easy to convince me that I'm making a fuss about nothing and so I asked the advice of a friend. He's the kind of enthusiast who owns multiple bikes worth more than my car and cycles in the wake of the Tour de France just because he can. Let's just say he is 'bemused' by my experience thus far, which has prompted me to contact you directly. Clearly your customer service department doesn't have the time and I'm loathed to go back to the store that sold me the bike.

Please will you answer a few questions honestly?

I weigh just under 10.5 stones (65kg) and, though I need to lose a few pounds, surely my mass hasn't broken the bike. With this morning's ride I have still clocked up less than 50 miles now since buying it, so I can't believe that I have worn the bike out through over zealous use.

Is this normal for a brand new bike?

Is this standard practice for Halfords? When I've bought bikes in the past and when I have replaced my inner tubes, I have always fitted them with tubes the correct diameter for the wheel. Is folding inner tubes Halfords policy? Is it normal for gears to go wrong so frequently? Are the grinding noises and loose units standard? Is it Halfords policy to try to 'get away with it', is it down to each store or did I simply buy a turkey? As I stated, whilst I would dearly love to spend more, I am not in a position to but I am wondering whether I wasted my money and should have continued my habit of buying cheap, old, disposable bikes.

I need to book my six-week service in a couple of weeks and I rather hope your staff might be kind enough to replace the inner tube with one the correct size and check the front wheel to ensure the correct inner tube has been fitted, but I am reluctant to return to Eastgate and one wonders what other shortcuts Halfords has taken and substandard products have been fitted to my bike.

Is it time to return the bike, ask for a refund and turn my back on Halfords for good? Please be honest with me. If I'm being unreasonable I'd like to know how and why. If I bought a poor bike I'd be intrigued to know why you sold it but, more importantly, I'd be grateful for your advice as to what I should consider in the future. If it is a Halfords issue, I'd like to know how we proceed and, if it is a combination of issues, I wonder if you would be kind enough to discuss my options with me.

I'll email this in a moment and post a hard copy to you later, just to be certain you receive it, and I shall look forward to hearing from you at your earliest convenience.

Yours sincerely.

Edward Field.

Case Study 2 – Halfords cont.

The response took a couple of days but I received two phone calls, from Matt, the store manager and John, the customer services team manager, and a plan to resolve the issue as quickly and smoothly as possible with a full service of the bike, replacement or a refund.

Uppermost in John's mind was ensuring a very negative experience was transformed into a positive experience and that I remained a content and loyal customer of Halfords. In the course of the telephone conversations John apologised, I outlined my frustrations and concerns and together we arranged possible solutions with John promising a phone call as soon as everything was in place. Certainly it is a shame that such a rapid escalation up the food chain was required from me, but it worked without need for anger or recriminations.

Or so I thought.

The promised phone call didn't materialise and a few days later the chairman's executive assistant dropped me an email, to which I fired off a curt response:

Dear Ms. ███

Thank you for responding to my email. John ██████ did indeed phone me on Thursday at 9.44 am. We spoke for 8 minutes and he assured me that he and Halfords would do "whatever it takes to turn a negative experience into a positive experience." He said he would arrange for the manager (Matt?) to be at the store when I arrived to talk through the issues and then arrange to either repair or replace the bike or give me a full refund. I responded that I was available on Friday afternoon or one day next week to suit Matt's schedule. Mr. ██████ made all the right noises, persuaded me that Halfords would make amends and asked me to wait while he phoned Matt to arrange a time, and assured me he would call me back "in about ten minutes."

Three days later I am still waiting.

Forgive me if I no longer have any faith in Halfords. In my experience of Halfords over the past few weeks, it is a company that sells shoddy goods, employs staff who, rather than use the correct sized components folds them and makes do, and fails to keep their word.

I think my relationship with Halfords is probably at an end. I am loath to make another twenty mile round trip just so that your staff can try to put right what should never have been wrong in the first place with a brand new bike. I shall remove the lights and water bottle etc. that I fitted to the bike and perhaps you could arrange for Mr. ██████ to pick the bike up from my house with a cheque for the full price I paid. In return I shall promise never to enter your shop again so that Halfords may continue under the illusion that its products and customer care are in good health.

I await your response in due course.

Yours sincerely.

Edward Field.

The following day I received another phone call from a contrite John. He had meant to call, been distracted and evidently it never happened. He apologised profusely and assured me that Halfords, he and Matt wanted desperately to see me satisfied. By that stage I had had enough and wanted only to receive a refund, get rid of the bike and chalk it up to experience. Reluctantly he accepted my decision and I returned the bike to the shop feeling dejected and very disappointed.

However, Matt and two of his staff members were waiting for me...

I'll fill in all the gaps with my final letter to Halfords in Chapter 9, Permission to Praise, but the short version is, though by that time all I wanted was to take the money (and no more) they owed me, Matt and his staff spent an hour with me, convinced me not only to accept an upgraded bike that they had already built ready for me as an apology from the store, but also to accept a full refund as stipulated by John and head office.

Success rating: 10/10 – *The gift of a free bike is stunning. It was way beyond my expectation and far removed from what I actually wanted by that stage. However, what impressed me most of all was the effort to which John, Matt and the team went in order to make amends - and then some! Their attitude was humbling and, though Halfords would have been one of the principal villains in this book had the saga concluded as I expected, their efforts have made Halfords as a whole and them as individuals the stand-out heroes. From their perspective, they now have a loyal customer who plans to purchase his next bike there, is planning on replacing his wife's bike with them, and now has no hesitation whatsoever in recommending Halfords and their Eastgate store, Bristol. Top marks and my eternal gratitude to them.*

And *that* is a very clear indication of the power of the written complaint and how verbal interaction compliments it perfectly.

Before we move on to selecting your victim (the recipient of your complaint), a word of warning: Fraudulent complaints and claims rarely end well. Don't do it! There are enough freebies in the world without lying, cheating and fabricating issues. If you find a dead mouse in your milk bottle (thank you Phillip Swain for that fantastic anecdote) then, yes, complain. Complain vociferously. But wanting a free cake is not justification for 'finding' a shard of rusty metal in your gateaux. Such fraudulent complaints can cost companies many thousands of pounds, which affects profits and can cause redundancies of innocent, hardworking staff. Just because you wanted a freebie. In reality, it is far more likely that in the ensuing investigation it will be discovered that the rusty shard originates not from the production line but from your garage and the resulting court case, fine or prison sentence will detrimentally alter the course of your life. Just because you wanted a freebie. Don't do it. Ever!

But if you are seeking a reason to complain legitimately and have thus far lived a charmed life where no ill has befallen you, fear not; I have sprinkled ideas, reasons and suggestions for you in Chapter 6, *Reasons to Rage*. Trust me, there is a genuine complaint waiting to happen with your name on it.

Chapter 3: Preparing for Battle

Enough is enough! Somebody did the dirty on you, the red mist has descended, the gloves are off and it's about to become very nasty. Nobody gets the better of you, right? How dare they ruin your day! The uncomfortable feeling inside that is churning your stomach, crawling across your skin and forcing steam from every orifice is the effect of your blood boiling at the audacity of their injustice. What are you going to do about it?

My advice? Calm down. Take a deep breath. Is any of this worth having a heart attack over? There are people starving, dying of horrible diseases, being persecuted by corrupt governments, oppressed by dark religions and abused by despicable humans; you have simply not received value for money or have been ill served. Before you seek justice you need to get the anger out of your system and put everything back into perspective. If you attack while you're angry, you will almost certainly fail in your cause. Aggression will only ever put someone's back up; anger will prevent you from thinking clearly, speaking or writing coherently and doom you to failure. I'm not saying that anger is wrong; on the contrary, I believe it is very healthy and perfectly normal, but it should be a process you go through and not the launch pad for your complaint.

Rage, but rage calmly, rationally and meaningfully.

In the course of a quarter of a century or so of complaining, I have spat venom, breathed fire and come unstuck on a few occasions. The last occasion was with Utility Warehouse and we'll get to that story in the next chapter. In my defence, the voice at the other end of the phone began shouting and swearing at me first and I'm afraid I then let rip. I won in the end because I had all the evidence on my side (more of that, too, in a moment) but at the end of that particular phone call, I was perspiring badly, shaking and I felt sick. It didn't ruin my day, but my wife opted for a very long walk while I climbed down from the ceiling. The resolution actually came with the next phone call and letter when I was calm and thinking clearly again.

You need to take your time in preparing for battle. If you burst in with all guns blazing, you are likely to discover you've forgotten something vital, you've made a mistake or you have confused yourself. If you are dealing with a customer service department or a manager it is almost certain they will have dealt with more problems than you, have a crib sheet next to their telephone and be very capable to tripping you up in your angry haste. Trust me on this, it is very embarrassing to discover the root of the problem is of your own doing and that there is no recourse but to apologise, hang up the phone and hide in the corner under a cloud of shame.

You can avoid the humiliation and failure of your complaint with a quick slap across the **CHoPPS**:

Clarity

Honesty

Preparation

Presentation

Solution

Let's deal with **clarity** first. Clarity is an essential tool in your complainer's toolkit. If you don't know exactly what went wrong and under what circumstances, how on earth are you going to convince anybody else to put it right? Before you get too riled, are you sure there is even a case to answer? Even if it is a spoof, the example of the Welsh customer who bought a pizza from Asda and phoned to complain there was no topping is a perfect example. Head over to YouTube and type in 'Asda pizza complaint' for the full, but brief, reason why clarity is imperative.

Idiocy aside, clarity brings us back to my earlier point about calming down and thinking through the problem. Relive the circumstances that have lead you to complain and talk them through with a family member or friend who is able to listen objectively, think rationally and confirm that you have a valid case or point out where there are gaps in your story. Get it right before you complain, not midway through your tirade.

And so to **honesty**. Take a breath. Count to ten. Breathe again. Right, is any of this *your* fault? Is any part of the problem caused by your mistake or a simple misunderstanding?

Go through everything again in your mind, slowly. Were you in the right shop? Did you buy or order the correct item? Did you read the instructions before using it? Did you break it through misuse? Did you fill out the form correctly? Did you write the correct time and date on the calendar? Were you taking all the precautions necessary and suggested to prevent the incident? Did you park correctly so that your rear wheel was clear of the dropped kerb?

It may be there is no case to answer and that it is just an unpleasant, expensive learning experience. Too many people refuse to take responsibility for their own actions and choose to blame someone else instead. Somebody very close to me overinflated the floor bladder on one of our inflatable kayaks recently in order to sit slightly higher in the water. Unfortunately, when she stood to climb out, the pressure split the valve. Yes, it is a weak point on the kayak and a design flaw on an otherwise perfectly good kayak but there was no blame to be apportioned to anyone else. It was our £70 mistake, not theirs.

However, sometimes you can be technically in the wrong and still make a valid complaint that is successful. In **Case Study 3**, I returned from a business trip in Sweden (via Copenhagen) and was delayed sufficiently to miss my train home. As my letter to First Great Western attests, I booked a seat on a specific train in order to obtain a better fare so as to save my employer money and so, according to the FGW's terms and conditions, I didn't have a leg to stand on. However, for me this was a matter not of legal obligations but of reason and humanity, both of which are frequently missing from FGW's customer relations, in my personal experience.

Case Study 3 – First Great Western

Through no fault of my own, I missed my train home. My presence on the later train did not adversely affect First Great Western, their profits or any of their other passengers and so I felt it was an issue of humanity and worthy of a scathing attack, particularly after previous run-ins with FGW (see Case Study 10 in Chapter 5, Blood from Stones*).*

Squircle Entertainment
Not quite a square; not quite a circle...

edward@squircleentertainment.com   www.squircleentertainment.com   www.squiss.co.uk
Squircle Entertainment,
+44 (0)   Twitter: @edwardsquircle

22 May 2014

Sir Chay Blyth, Chairman
First Great Western
Head Office
Milford House
1, Milford Street
Swindon
SN1 1HL

Dear Sir Chay

Last night I attempted to catch the 22:15 train home from London Paddington to Bristol Temple Meads. It is a journey I take frequently and I tend to book my tickets prior to my journey and select an Advance Saver return. However, upon landing at Heathrow (from Copenhagen) the ground crew 'forgot' to arrive to release us from the aeroplane. They then took an inordinate period of time to release our baggage, with the consequence that I missed two possible Heathrow Express trains and arrived about three minutes after my train had departed, rather than the expected thirty minutes early.

Despite the 23:30 train being virtually empty (I counted four other people in the quiet carriage with me), I was forced to pay an additional £31.50 for a new ticket home, by a brusque and officious train manager (I'm afraid I did not catch her name).

Whilst I accept that the ticket I bought was for a particular train, the object of the rule she enforced is to prevent passengers from purchasing cheap off-peak tickets and travelling on peak-time services when demand is highest. Through no fault of my own, I missed my train; a regular service that is many hours after peak time and never even remotely full in my experience. I was forced to catch a less convenient train, which had even fewer passengers and was even more hours outside the peak-time restrictions.

Do you select your staff on their ability to steadfastly refuse to see reason, to lack any hint of understanding or compassion, to utterly eschew customer care and to scrabble around to snatch as many grubby pounds as possible for your greedy company? I have no choice over train services; I am forced to use First Great Western but I resent every penny your overzealous staff gleefully filches from me.

I would be grateful if you would see reason and refund the cost of my unnecessary additional ticket.

Yours sincerely,

Edward Field.

Success rating: 7/10 – *My letter was passed to Mark Webber, Customer Relations Senior Officer and, though he reiterated that the train manager was in the right to charge me the full price for another ticket, he appreciated my frustration and* *credited my account with £31.50 to cover the ticket price.*

Honesty isn't just about admitting one's own failings, it is also about telling the truth. *Be sure your sin will find you out.* There isn't much you can get away with nowadays. There are cameras everywhere and no matter what you say, what you do or where you go, there is a very good chance that someone is aware of and recording your actions. To lie or cheat in order to make financial gain is fraud. I know I mentioned it in the previous chapter but it is essential that it sinks in. Call it karma, call it justice, but if you are dishonest, eventually it will come back to bite you on the bum. A desire for honesty and to do the right thing in life *should* be enough, however for the cynics amongst you there have been plenty of occasions when I have been in the wrong, I have told the truth and I have been rewarded for it.

In February 2008 I drove a van for a job around the North Circular to Watford. I was unfamiliar with the road at the time and so was conscious of the variable speed restrictions, ensuring I drove 2mph below the requirement for each stretch. I was stunned when a double flash indicated I had exceeded the limit and the resulting letter informed me I was 8mph over the limit. There was no point in lying but I wrote to the Operational Command Unit of the Metropolitan Police explaining that I had driven carefully and that, as I had not seen the sign indicating the reduction from 50mph to 40mph I could only assume it had been blocked by one of the many goods vehicles I had overtaken at that time of the morning.

I was in the wrong, but I believe my absolute honesty worked in my favour and I received a letter informing me that no further action would be taken and the fine rescinded but that it would be advisable to take a little more care in future. Result, and no need for lies or deception!

Now that you have established there is a case and you know exactly what it is, it's time to decide what format your complaint takes and how to structure it. **Preparation** is key to ensuring the final presentation of your complaint is clear enough for even the most obtuse customer service operative to understand and simple enough to you to present.

Let's start with the telephone complaint. Grab a pen and paper and make notes of all the relevant information for which you will be asked and the questions you have:

- Where/when/how did it happen?
- What did/didn't occur that should/shouldn't have?
- Who was the cause of your upset?
- To whom were you referred?
- Why are you upset?
- What were you expecting/paying for?
- What was the cost to you (in money, time, offence etc.)?

- How do you want this resolved?
- What is the timescale for resolution?
- If it fails, how/when should you follow up?

Next, copy and print the Telephone Complaint Log from *The Complainer's Toolkit* in Chapter 7.

Sometimes you may be fortunate enough to have to make only one phone call in order for your complaint to be resolved satisfactorily. More often than not you will make multiple calls to numerous people and your reasons to complain will increase exponentially. As you are passed from department to department and the promised return calls never materialise you will need a detailed log as reference so that you can fight the bureaucratic machine. It is essential that you log the date and time of every phone call you make, the duration (you may want to claim for the cost of each call), the person or people to whom you speak, the assurances given, promises made and timeline for the expected resolution so that you can refer to it in each subsequent phone call.

Telephone operatives for large companies are generally instructed to record all the details of the calls they receive. Whether they do or not, if *you* have recorded all the details it will immediately wrong-foot them and set you in good stead to achieve your goals. If you can bombard them with facts to which they have no defence or confirm everything they have also recorded, they are less likely to contradict you or wish to cross you when it gets down to the nitty-gritty of recompense. Blind them with science (and truth) and they will want to resolve the issue and be rid of you as swiftly and painlessly as possible.

I'm going to lump email and letter writing together as the principles are the same; only the means of delivery should be different. Because emails are simpler to send, it is far easier for you to make mistakes and regret them before you have had time to review your words, so write them as a letter first and then attach *and* paste them into your email.

Once you have completed your checklist of the whats, whys and wheres of your complaint, you will need to know where to send your email and letter. Chapter 4, *Organ Grinders & Monkeys*, deals with the specifics of target selection but as a general rule envelopes addressed to 'To Whom It May Concern' or to the customer service department in general are less likely to be approached with care and most likely to enter the large pile of complaints that eventually receive the generic 'We care, have £5 off your next purchase and go away' responses.

Next, confirm the recipient's address. I know this sounds obvious, but again I have witnessed some absolute clangers. As with any letter, using the correct street, number and postcode makes life a great deal easier for the postal workers but, before you deal with those specifics, do you have the correct town? What about the country?

If you just found half a slug in the burger you bought from your local junk outlet you probably have the option of writing to the manager of that branch, somebody important at the UK head office (or in whichever country you bought the burger and are reading this book), or the biggest big cheeses at the central hub of it all in the USA (do they own *all* the burger joints in town...?). Different complaints may be handled better by different offices so one rule doesn't necessarily apply.

Ensure you have the correct title, job description and spelling of your victim's name; it isn't a good start if they are bristling before they even reach the first paragraph. Usually you can find the contact details on each company's website. Most will have a 'Contact Us' page, but bear in mind that is where and how they *want* you to submit your complaints and enquiries, which may not always be the best option for you.

There are numerous company directories out there either at your library or online and, if all else fails, the modern rule of research works here: *Google is your friend.* You may need to be creative with your research but it will be worth it if you can put your letter in the hands of the person with the power and authority to deal with it and improve your world.

Ready? Telephone in hand? Computer booted? Pen primed? It's **Presentation** time!

If you are phoning, remember to be calm and polite. It is very unlikely that the poor soul at the other end of the line, at least to start with, is in any way responsible for your annoyance. It is not their fault you are upset, that you had to wait in a queue on the phone, that you despise the automated switchboards, that they are in a call centre in a different country, that they are not able to resolve your problems instantly... They are quite possibly earning little more than minimum wage and would far prefer to be sunning themselves on a beach than listening to your woes. If you allow your emotions to enter into the conversation with them, it will cloud your judgment, you will trip yourself up and, if you end up yelling at them, you may find yourself listening to a dialing tone and will have to begin the whole process from scratch.

Don't waste time. If you didn't heed my advice in Chapter 2, *Pick Your Fights, Set Your Sights*, and save time by using **PleasePress1**, why not? Select, or ask to be put through to, the correct department. If you are asked "What is it concerning?", don't waste your time and breath on the full saga at this stage. A simple "The kettle I bought from you just exploded, my kitchen is now missing and I need to speak with the person responsible," will suffice. Save your energy for the person who deserves your ire. It is very unlikely that the next voice you hear will be that of the CEO, but you should at least hear a department manager in your ear who will know how to deal with the situation and escalate it if necessary. If not, and they fob you off, insist on speaking with somebody who is in the position to deal with a lawsuit. That usually works for me.

Using your notes and maintaining your composure in spite of the puerile questions they will inevitably ask and the lack of comprehension they may display, explain the situation in chronological order. Although you may still be upset about having been kept waiting, don't mention it. It is in the past, is not related to your complaint, is an emotional issue and will mark you out as a whinger rather than a customer with a legitimate complaint.

Don't swear and don't raise your voice; it will only hinder you. Speak clearly and slowly, particularly if you or they have an accent or are struggling to understand. If you tend to lose your words, refer to your notes. I frequently jot down phrases that I want to use but might slip out of my mind when the conversation doesn't flow as I expect.

Use the manager's name when appropriate. It builds the relationship and makes it far more personal and that way s/he will invest more time and effort in resolving the issue. For the same reason, I ask them to call me 'Edward' rather than 'Mr. Field.' It is easier to for them to connect with me and care about me if on first name terms.

How many times have you heard the phrase 'we may record this conversation' when phoning a company? I always play them at their own game. I have never actually recorded a telephone conversation myself but if I suspect it will be a challenging process I ask them to ensure the call *is* recorded. They may not record it and you will have no control over the matter, but it does make it very clear that you are to be taken seriously, it implies that you are recording (or taking detailed notes) as evidence and, when they are uncaring or flippant in their handling of your complaint, I find it really puts the willies up them. It is a gentle way of saying "Don't mess with me because I know exactly what I'm doing and I am so convinced I am in the right that I want to make sure you have all the evidence and cannot escape it."

At the culmination of your conversation, even if they are passing you on to somebody else, confirm their name, email address and direct number, and let them know kindly but firmly that you are holding them responsible for resolving your issue and that you will use their name in future correspondence and contact them directly if promises are broken and the situation unresolved. This puts pressure on them to deal with the issue swiftly and effectively and also gives you a point of reference and evidence if you need to move further up the food chain.

Letter writing is an art form. Anyone can throw words at a page but few can do so eloquently, stylishly and with maximum effect. I'm not saying I can, but I give it a jolly good go. I'm not going to teach you where to position the addresses or the rules of grammar; many of these rules change over time. At various stages I was taught to write my address either in a block or with each line indented further than the previous line. I was also taught to sign off with 'Yours sincerely' if I had used the recipient's name, and 'Yours faithfully' if I had addressed it 'To Whom It May Concern'. Rules change and fashions vary. I don't believe the layout of the letter is a 'make or break' matter nowadays, just as long as it is clear, neat and presents you as intelligent and erudite. First impressions *do* count and you will be judged on the appearance and presentation of your letter as much as the content.

If you are uncertain, there are many, many resources online that explain how to compose different styles of letter and the correct layout for each. I've included various websites and resources in Chapter 7, *The Complainer's Toolkit*, but be warned, there are few cast iron rules and you will find differences across the various websites. I would suggest you find one or two sources that you like and stick with them. Don't get too hung up on the minutiae of letter writing if it doesn't come naturally to you.

That said, if you have not yet grasped the principals of sentence construction, have a very limited understanding of grammar and your spelling is ~~atroshus~~, ~~atrotious~~, really bad I would urge you to make a friend of your computer spell-checker and ask somebody you can rely on to proofread your letter before you send it. I cringe when I spot a typo in my letter *after* I have sent it (see if you can find those in the letters in this book) and my confidence wavers when I receive responses riddled with spelling mistakes and grammatical errors. If the person dealing with my complaint cannot be bothered to check the spelling in their letter, what chance do I have of them caring enough about the bigger issues, like resolving my complaint? Do you want the recipient to disregard you because your presentation is a joke to them?

In the same vein, if your handwriting is appalling, don't do it. Mine has often been described as resembling the aftermath of a spider running across the page with ink on its feet. Consequently I use a computer and save the pen for my own private notes.

There are certain letter writing 'truths' that I believe are open to discussion. The general opinion is that a handwritten letter should be in blue or black ink. Apparently red ink is for angry teachers, purple ink is for sexually repressed witches and green ink is for the freaks and nut jobs of the world. However, whilst I 'write' my letters on a computer, just occasionally I take a warped pleasure in signing my name in green ink and wondering how much it concerns the recipients.

Likewise, writing your letters in BLOCK CAPITALS, particularly if in a **BOLD** font or **ENLARGED AND COLOURED TO *REALLY* UPSET THE RECIPIENT** is probably not a good idea if you don't want them to consider sending you a jacket with buckles on the back. It's a good truth, generally speaking, although there have been a couple of very rare and particularly necessary occasions where I have written a sentence in bold, block capitals and even with a touch of underlining. Rest assured, that was as far as I went.

The example that springs to mind was back in 1998. I was working for a post-production company in Soho, London as a runner on £8,000 p.a. having just graduated from the Bristol Old Vic Theatre School. As there were no grants available to me, I had funded myself through two years of school with multiple jobs, a major fundraising campaign and some very generous charitable trust donations. I made up the shortfall with a Career Development Loan from Barclays Bank, which was supposed to be repaid upon graduation at a set monthly rate of about £200. On my salary and living in London, that just wasn't possible. I survived the first two years there by eating the clients' leftovers for lunch and staying late in the office to eat fruit and Marmite on toast in the evenings.

I applied to Barclays Bank for a payment deferment but was rejected. I wrote to the correct department explaining my situation and was again rejected. When I phoned to plead my case, the officious, arrogant man on the other end damned me. He took great delight in telling me he was going to ruin my credit rating, bankrupt me, send the bailiffs around to seize all my possessions and destroy the career that the very loan I had taken out with Barclays was supposed to have launched. The telephone call almost brought me to tears as I thought my life was about to crumble.

I responded immediately with a two-page, heartfelt and brutally honest letter to the head of the Career Development Loan department outlining my situation and the man's threats. I pleaded for help and included in my second paragraph the following:

I DID <u>NOT</u> AT ANY POINT, NOR HAVE I <u>EVER</u> STATED OR IMPLIED THAT I INTEND TO AVOID REPAYING MY LOAN. On the contrary, as the recording [of my conversation] will prove, during the conversation I stated I do intend to repay it in full.

I followed the letter up two days later with a phone call, reached the manager, gave him my name and began my explanation. He stopped me and said, "Hold on a moment. Was yours the letter with the block capital sentence? Let me find it and call you back..."

Though not a device I would use now or encourage, it had absolutely the desired effect: it stood out as a desperate, panicky shout for help and reason. And it worked. One man lost his job, another was given a stay of execution with his loan and the department manager ensured that Barclays Bank genuinely helped launch a career.

As an addendum to that, writing letters in wax crayon is always inadvisable unless you are under the age of three or in a 10 x 6 cell and a danger to yourself.

If at all possible, address the recipient by name and use his/her title. If they've earned a knighthood or life peerage, don't insult them by referring to them as Mr. or Ms. You might well be frustrated but you need them on your side. If the correspondence continues across several letters and they sign off with only their forename, you can make a judgment call on whether to address them as such in future. I tend to continue using *their* titles until the letters have lightened in tone as the resolution is close or if we have conversed on the phone and used first names. Just as using forenames makes the matter far more personal, it is harder to step back to the formality of Mr. and Ms. if further problems arise.

Present your letter clearly so that it is easy to follow the chronology of the complaint. Do you remember science classes where your teacher insisted upon the standard format of Aim, Apparatus, Method, Results and Conclusion? Writing a letter of complaint is just as formulaic:

Introduction – Who you are and why you are complaining. One paragraph will usually suffice.

Explanation – What went wrong, why it happened, what upset you and the chronology of the incident or incidents. Usually this is the bulk of the letter, particularly if it is an ongoing saga.

Reasoning – Why this should not have happened and what you would have expected from the transaction or experience ordinarily. Again, one paragraph should clear that up.

Results – what you expect them to do about it, the timescale you expect it to be completed within and the repercussions if they fail. If that won't fit into a paragraph I would suggest your demands are a little excessive.

Conclusion – Your parting shot and signature. Brief.

Be very careful with the language and style that you use. Writing in the style of Charles Dickens is unlikely to do you any favours unless you are complaining to the Folio Society about their latest publication of *A Tale of Two Cities*. Equally don't be too casual or flippant if you wish to be taken seriously.

Just as you should refrain from swearing when complaining by telephone, avoid using expletives in your letter unless you are repeating verbatim an insult that you have suffered, and only then if it is imperative to the case. I was taught that the use of expletives is an indication of a limited vocabulary and a lack of intelligence. In later life I have discovered the art of swearing sparingly and for effect (sometimes a punch-line is flat without the right expletive) but as a general rule obscenities have no place in letters of complaint.

Colloquialisms are also best eschewed. There can be confusion with their meaning, and why would you project yourself as a person ignorant of the correct words when the outcome depends very much on whether the recipient of your letter respects you? The next rule applies more to the younger generation: Don't use textspeak! OMG! IMHO no1 is going 2 take u seriously if u complain like this. Their reply is likely 2 b a simple: O well, SH!

And in case you haven't worked it out for yourself, emoticons are absolutely

forbidden!

Don't threaten; promise. If you threaten to take a particular action unless the wrongdoer takes a certain course and they decline, you are then faced with either having to carry out your threat completely or crawling away with an awful lot of egg smeared across your face. If the thought of going to court scares you, don't threaten it. If you don't have the balls to contact the Jeremy Vine show and risk being invited on as a guest, don't play that card. Telling British Airways that, unless they find your lost suitcase and refund all your expenses, you will 'go public' is an empty threat unless you are fully prepared to do so. And, yes, I did!

The risks of going public are two-fold: Firstly, there is the distinct possibility of attention and scrutiny from the press, social media and whichever ombudsman is responsible for the industry that has upset you and, if you have not been entirely truthful or have confused the facts, you may be exposed on a grand scale. Today's newspapers being tomorrow's chip wrappings is a thing of the past. Once it is online and in the public domain, it is there for ever and ever and ever...

Secondly, something *will* happen. That something is hopefully a resolution with which you are completely satisfied, but it may be an escalation in a direction you were not expecting, are not at ease with and exposes you to unwelcome repercussions. Be warned and be careful.

Threatening to take your custom elsewhere is the easiest threat to make, is often the least effective and usually the most inconvenient for you if it goes awry.

They probably don't need your money as much as you depend on their service or product. Don't shoot yourself in the foot with a threat you are not truly prepared to carry out but may be forced to. Unless you are currently ranked on the Sunday Times Rich List, informing your bank that they must sort out the mess they have made with your bank charges within twenty-four hours or you will close your account is not going to bother them in the slightest. Why would they care about your overdraft? And how much grief is it going to cause *you* to find another bank and transfer your standing orders, direct debits, inform the payroll department and wait for new bank cards?

Public humiliation, however... Now *there's* a weapon against ineptitude and injustice!

But before I give you that case study, an addendum to my rule *Tell the truth*. Don't lie, don't *ever* lie. Sometimes, however, a little embellishment or a certain skewing of the story adds sufficient spice to make your complaint stand out from usual humdrum letters customer service departments receive. If it doesn't flow naturally from your pen or mind, leave it to someone else, but if you have a dark streak of flare and imagination then it can work wonders for your cause. Rein yourself in, though. Don't make your adaptation of the saga so extreme as to be unrealistic, or so sarcastic as to be offensive. For me, whilst I don't like being put in the position of having to complain and would far prefer an easy, hassle-free life, when there *is* need to complain and it hasn't caused me serious upset or inconvenience, I see it as an opportunity for some fun.

Case Study 4 – British Airways

*My stomach sank as the baggage carousel emptied and I remained, watching the same few bags go round and round and watching my own dismay replicated in the faces of the other few passengers awaiting their own cases. For some it was a major issue but for me it was a minor annoyance; better on the return trip than on the outward journey. Besides, this promised to be one of my most enjoyable, most effective and most public complaints to date. A faceless company such as British Airways with a reputation for losing baggage and not really giving a fig about it was far more likely to act upon a humorous, embarrassing public rant than a meek, private letter. I had my own website, **www.squiss.co.uk**, and I was going to make damn sure they couldn't ignore me...*

Squircle Entertainment

Not quite a square; not quite a circle...

edward@squircleentertainment.com
Squircle Entertainment, ██████████████████

www.squircleentertainment.com

+44 (0)██████████

Twitter: @edwardsquircle

Blog: www.squiss.co.uk

8 June 2013

Sir Martin Broughton, Chairman & Keith Williams, CEO
British Airways
Waterside
Speedbird Way
off Bath Road
Harmondsworth
UB7 0GA

martin███████████com
keith███████████com

Dear Sir Martin & Mr Williams

Last night I won first prize in British Airways' baggage competition! I am delighted to report I won a tiny stick of deodorant, some shower gel, a flimsy toothbrush, one portion of toothpaste (for those who don't like to clean their teeth at night *and* in the morning) and an XL white t-shirt, which my wife and I should be able to wear simultaneously.

I think I did rather well considering the entry price was just three taxi rides, a suitcase, clothes, a wash bag, car keys...

On the bright side, my luggage is enjoying a mystery trip while I am still in possession of the socks I worked and travelled in yesterday. Hurrah!

For some reason, which was never fully explained, our 21:45 flight (BA0401) from Brussels to Heathrow was delayed by about an hour. Then, a little over an hour later, BA ramped up the excitement substantially when not one but two of the extending walkways failed to extend to allow my fellow passengers and I to alight. I can assure you the banter on board was both jocular and very complimentary. Whilst the enjoyment ended there for most of the passengers, I was fortunate to be one of six specially selected winners who were awarded quality time together around the luggage carousel watching the empty spaces grow as cases were removed and ours failed to take their places. Mystifyingly, five cases and a rucksack remained upon the carousel long after all the other passengers had trundled home and one wonders what you did with the owners. Even I am in awe at your ability to lose humans as successfully as inanimate objects.

I have to admit, the British Airways staff member who handed out our prizes and issued claim forms was entirely sympathetic declaring, "*Six* of you? Wow! Usually it's only one or two..."

The way she made the statement reminded me of a certain rail company that, a few years ago, issued a self-congratulatory statement that "*fewer* of our trains now drive through red lights" and expected us to celebrate heartily with them.

Assuming your representative meant 'one or two cases per flight' and that each of your 256 aircraft (according to Wikipedia) fly just once per day, 365 days per year, that's still somewhere between 93,440 and 186,800 pieces of baggage that take impromptu holidays without their owners every year. Would you like us to congratulate you audibly or will my written best wishes suffice?

But I digress and I'd hate you to think this letter is all about *you*.

With my special British Airways prize bag in hand, I departed Terminal 5 at approximately 00:20 (about 90 minutes later than anticipated) to catch my transfer to the hotel only to discover I had missed the last bus by 45 minutes. Filled with prize-winning joy, I returned to the concourse in the hope of finding a member of BA staff to share my joy with and enquire about a bolt-on reward in the form of transport to my bed. Alas, from its reported revenue of approximately €13.6 billion, BA has decided it is more fun to leave its prize-winners stranded with nary a help desk operative in evidence after office hours. I'm not going to question the wisdom of abandoning your passengers at a time when the airport also closes its help desks as it's obviously more amusing to leave them to stew for several hours.

I'm sure you're anxious to know that my six hours at the Travelodge passed without any excitement, other than my pleasant shower followed by the replacement of my socks that were ripe enough to be making their own bid for freedom.

Upon arrival in Bristol, however, I discovered how challenging it is to drive one's car home when the keys are at a mystery location somewhere distinctly *not* Bristol. Thank goodness for taxis that make twenty-mile round trips to the village in which I live (and keep the spare key) for a mere £44 (making that a £79 donation to taxi drivers, thanks to BA).

Sidetracking slightly, a few years ago my bank refused to accept my claims that I had moved home and persisted in sending my bank statements to a stranger. When they finally conceded that I was in fact correct and *did* know where I lived, they apologised profusely for the months of ineptitude and sent me a very generous Fortnum and Mason hamper.

Naturally, I don't expect an apology from British Airways as I'm well aware of your reputation for not giving two hoots about your passengers and your reluctance to take responsibility when service goes awry, although if you do feel so inclined, hampers are rather *passé* and I'd prefer tickets to the royal box for this year's Wimbledon men's final (for myself and my fellow prize-winners) and a directorship at Watford FC (that one's just mine!). However, I *do* think a gift of £79 to cover my expenses is the absolute least you should offer.

At this juncture I still don't have my suitcase but I'm hopeful my luggage will tire of its own trip soon and return to me swiftly. Naturally, if life *sans* owner is preferable to it I shall contact you again for a further donation to cover the cost of my suits, shoes, keys, toiletries, fresh socks...

On a final note, I would like to defend British Airways and declare that I find it unfathomable that, with service and prizes such as this, why so many of us prefer to fly Virgin Atlantic. That said, next week when you fly me to Copenhagen for another job, would you mind awarding the prize to someone else?

Yours sincerely

Edward Field.

Success rating: 7/10 – *The open letter, which I uploaded to my **Essays & Diatribes** page on the website, became my most successful posting. I received a full refund for my expenses and my BA account was credited with 15,000 Avios points. It wasn't the Wimbledon tickets or the Watford directorship I was hoping for, but it* *was a great deal better than nothing and I enjoyed the process of writing my open letter and the response it achieved immensely.*

Whilst I certainly had a dig at British Airways, I refrained from being outright insulting. It does not serve your purpose to attack the subject of your letter. Often pointed questions lead to a more positive outcome than damning statements. Generally speaking it is best to avoid the insults, but if you *are* going to insult a company or its bigwigs, do so cleverly, wittily and with panache. Calling somebody 'big nose' or 'nobjob' may well help you let off steam but it is not going to endear you to them. On the other hand, asking the CEO of a multi-national corporation that has failed repeatedly to resolve your issue why s/he presides over a staff of morons may not be entirely accurate but it does get the depth of your feeling across quite clearly. Not that I have ever been quite so direct, of course.

There are occasions when humour just won't do. Sometimes it is necessary to vent, to politely but emphatically express one's extreme displeasure at the service provided. In all instances of letter writing, and in these particularly, I would urge you not to post your first draft in haste but to sleep on it, reread it and edit it the following day. Once you have posted the letter or email, there is no going back. I am ashamed to admit that I ignored all of my rules a couple of years ago when, on a particularly awful bad hair day, I was given cause to write to TD Direct Investing yet again:

Case Study 5 – TD Direct Investing

It needs no introduction. Just read it and feel my shame.

Squircle Entertainment

Not quite a square; not quite a circle...

edward@squircleentertainment.com   www.squircleentertainment.com
Squircle Entertainment,
+44 (0)   Twitter: @edwardsquircle

14 January 2013

Department of the Utterly Inept
TD Direct Investing (Europe) Ltd.
Exchange Court
Duncombe Street
Leeds
LS1 4AX

To Whom It May Concern:

Reference Account: 0

This is at least my fifth contact with you regarding this matter.

CHANGE MY ADDRESS, YOU UTTER MORONS!

Further to every other email, phone call and letter, I STILL moved house in September 2011. Why can you not see fit to send my mail to *me* rather than whoever now lives at 20, ███████████, Bristol, BS██████?

Deal with it!

Yours faithfully

Edward Field.

Success rating: 5/10 – *There is no excuse, but I had had enough. I should have stopped, rethought and written a far more polite letter the following day. That said, it did the trick. You should have seen the toady letter I received in response.*

Congratulations, you have hung up, pressed send, dropped the letter in the postbox, your presentation absolutely rocked. What could possibly go wrong with the **solution**?

In my experience, more often than not, one letter does the job. The voucher arrives, the matter is forgotten and it is time to move on with my life until the next campaign arises. The solution is perfect. Thank you very much indeed.

But life would be tedious if everything always worked out smoothly. Just occasionally *they*, the bureaucrats, the faceless suits, the bored, lazy, uncaring customer service staff contrive to 'lose' your letter of complaint in the hope you might disappear and save them the bother of having to clear up the mess. The solution to their non-solutions is simple: Complain again and complain more vociferously.

Sometimes the solution offered doesn't cut the mustard. There have been occasions when I have had the distinct impression that I have been patronized and fobbed off. Sometimes the reward is sufficient enough for me not to care, but once in a while it plucks at a nerve with a sharpened talon, my horns grow, my tongue sharpens and I feel a compulsion to enter the fray again. And this time there will be no survivors.

There was a time when family and friends exhaled and shook their heads when they heard of each new complaint. I recall my friend and brother-in-law, Matt, once sighing and asking "Why do you bother? Why not let it go? You waste so much time dealing with complaints, and time is money."

His comments came after a particularly good week and I took great delight in responding, "Because last week I wrote letters that resulted in the cancelling of a speeding fine, the reimbursement of unjust bank charges, a £50 credit from one bank and a Fortnum and Mason hamper from another. I'd say that was pretty good for four hours work."

Ever since, I have been his 'go to guy' when he has had need to complain and **Case Study 6** was one such letter I wrote for him that perfectly illustrates the situation of a solution being wholly unsatisfactory and the need for a second attack...

Case Study 6 – Tesco

To have more impact, I wrote these letters as Matt, rather than try a 'my brother-in-law says you mistreated his wife...' approach. There was no need for embellishment here and I made my position and annoyance abundantly clear.

Matt Sims

22 December 2010

Terry Leahy, CEO
Tesco
Tesco House
Delamare Road
Cheshunt
Hertfordshire
EN89SL

terry███████████com

Dear Mr Leahy

Re: Delivery Order ████████ Clubcard No. ████████████

I wish to report to you and complain about the ineptitude, incompetence, poor customer service, inadequate communication, appalling treatment and lies that my wife has suffered from Tesco.

My wife, Ronnie, placed a substantial order with you several weeks ago, for delivery yesterday, knowing that demand for delivery slots would be high, inclement weather was expected and that she would not have time to shop in person so close to Christmas. Indeed, ALL other delivery slots have been booked for over two weeks.

Ronnie arranged delivery for yesterday, Tuesday 21st December, between 17:00 and 19:00 hours. Yesterday morning, she was alerted that the delivery may be slightly late due to the adverse weather conditions. Naturally this was not an issue at all. However, at 14:39, Ronnie received a text stating: *We are very sorry we have had to cancel your order today due to bad weather. Please replace your order at Tesco.com when conditions in your area improve.*

We, and our neighbours, have been driving carefully on our roads without any issue, despite the snow. We have not suffered additional snow or ice for two days and the roads have not deteriorated, but improved, in that time. I must also reiterate that it was impossible to replace the order as there are no further slots available.

When Ronnie phoned the Brislington store directly to see if the delivery could be made at a later time yesterday, she was told quite bluntly that it would be impossible due to the conditions. She was advised, however, to drive herself to the store to shop *using the very same roads!* Ronnie further enquired whether the order could be prepared so that she could quickly collect it and return home but was informed that would also be impossible due to a, and I quote, "severe shortage of staff."

As I have been working away, my wife, who was at home with four children aged between 6 months and 10 years old, one of whom was ill, was expected to take all four children to the store to complete the order that filled two trolleys, because the weather and a *severe shortage of staff* prevented Tesco from fulfilling its duty to a loyal customer.

With no other option, my wife was forced to pay £50 for a last-minute babysitter to look after the children for the three-and-a-half hours it took for the door-to-door trip. The task was made considerably harder because the order, when printed out, was randomly complied without any logic or reference to departments within the store. Surely this in itself is an issue that can be easily rectified by Tesco's technology!

Once at the Brislington store, Ronnie was assisted by a very considerate member of staff, Jason, who informed her that there was, and had been, absolutely no shortage of staff whatsoever on the day, evening or night shifts and that, contrary to claims made over the phone, the staff were *not* overworked and the shop was relatively quiet. It would appear that the roads and weather conditions had *not* prevented any staff from arriving for their shifts! Indeed, the delivery could have been made or, at the very least, the order could have been prepared with ease for her to collect.

Upon arriving home, she also discovered that other supermarkets *in addition to Tesco* had in fact made deliveries to Walsh Avenue, just one road over from ours and only a couple of hours before our delivery was due. Needless to say, there has been no deterioration in the weather conditions since those deliveries were made.

Furthermore, a close friend of ours contacted Tesco upon hearing of Ronnie's plight to find out if her delivery would be made. She was informed that the delivery would go ahead as booked, that there was absolutely no problem and that Tesco had missed only one delivery all week! It does not take great powers of deduction to establish that the only order that Tesco has failed to honour this week is that of my wife!

All this leads to a few challenging questions for you:

Why was there just one window in an entire week when Tesco found it impossible to deliver the much-needed groceries to my wife and four children?

Why did the weather prevent Tesco from delivering to just one house, which is on a busy estate, in the whole of Bristol when, according to staff and other customers, it did not in any way hinder or prevent any staff from arriving at work or *any* other deliveries *in the whole of Bristol* being made this week?

Why do you employ telephone staff who are either deluded about the reality of weather conditions and delivery requirements or simply liars?

Why do the very same staff claim the roads are too dangerous for trained drivers to make deliveries but perfectly safe for tired, pressured mums to drag four young children out of the home to drive along?

What can my wife possibly have done to Tesco to be treated in such an offensive and appalling manner?

Why did Tesco select my wife and children out of the entirety of Bristol to emphatically refuse to assist in any way with a delivery or preparation of her order for her to collect and then add insult to injury by lying to her?

What exactly are you as a representative of Tesco going to do to make amends?

I am intrigued to hear how you can possibly defend and justify the actions of your company and staff and expect to hear from you by return post or, preferably, courier with adequate explanation, apology and recompense for her treatment and suffering.

Yours sincerely

Matt Sims.

The response from Tesco was far from satisfactory and this was very clearly a situation that needed a more fervent attack:

Matt Sims

4 January 2011

Terry Leahy, CEO
Tesco
Tesco House
Delamare Road
Cheshunt
Hertfordshire
EN89SL

terry█████████.com

Dear Sir Terry

Re: Delivery Order █████ **Clubcard No.** █████████████

I must begin by apologizing for omitting your correct title in my previous email to you.

Thank you for the reply written by Fiona ████. I am sorry that you didn't feel that I was worthy of your attention and personal response but, alas, this is what we, the customers who keep large companies in business, have come to accept as the norm in this society. Whilst I am grateful that my grievance has been acknowledged I am extremely dissatisfied by the response and solution offered by Tesco on your behalf.

Firstly, Fiona states that 'every effort' was made to make the deliveries. Either this is a blatant lie or your store-based staff is inept and lacks the interest to be resourceful and solve small problems. As the former Managing Director of a multi-national event management company, it was necessary to resolve issues as they unexpectedly occurred in order to maintain my excellent client relationship and ensure that external circumstances did not impeded the success of their shows, conferences and events, irrespective of the monetary value. An extreme example of this was the failure of a shipping company to sail an entire stage and set across to the Middle East for a major product launch. With just two days before the show was due to start, we discovered that the ship was still several days away from the port. I value my clients and failure was, and is, *never* an option and so we solved the problem by bringing in a Royal Navy Chinook helicopter from an aircraft carrier to lift the container off the ship and fly it to Abu Dhabi poste-haste.

To put this into context, Tesco had to solve the issue of delivering my wife's much-needed groceries. Whilst I accept that, unfathomably, the order was due to be delivered from the Midsomer Norton store some 12 miles away, I fail to understand why nobody considered that a phone call to the Brislington store, that also stocks groceries, a mere 3 miles away would be a very simple solution. Can you explain how I can recruit the Royal Navy and yet you cannot deliver a grocery order from a close, and perfectly accessible, branch of your own company to a home three miles away through clear roads?

Secondly, Fiona alludes to the 'confusion' caused. This wasn't simply a matter of confusion, my wife was misled at best, lied to at worst and, undeniably, subject to mild verbal abuse and a complete breakdown in customer relations.

Finally, Fiona proffered a £20 e-coupon 'by way of an apology for any disappointment caused.' *Disappointment*? How dare you belittle my wife's stressful predicament as *disappointing*! Do you have any concept of the anxiousness a mum of four young children feels at a time of such pressure when her husband is away on business, one of the children is sick, three are tired and just regular young children and there is nobody around to help her? My wife, as with many, many mums in her position in the real world, depends on the grocery delivery to make just one aspect of her daily routine a little easier. You failed her. Tesco's ineptitude, lack of caring, consideration, planning, foresight and a complete inability to solve a simple problem was not merely disappointing. It was distressing, time-consuming, costly and heaped additional stress and pressure on a young mum of four who was trying to manage a family, a home and all that goes with it at the busiest time of year.

A £20 e-coupon might well compensate mere disappointment but it does *not* cover the £50 babysitting fees incurred or make amends for the wanton disregard for my wife's predicament, the offence and stressed caused her or Tesco's utter ineptitude.

I wait your personal response, Sir Terry.

Yours sincerely

Matt Sims.

Success rating: 8/10 – *Sir Terry's response was personal, swift and very apologetic. Whilst he endeavoured to explain the situation, he conceded that it was unacceptable and that the inconvenience to Ronnie was unacceptable. He also enclosed a £50 Tesco Moneycard, bringing the total compensation to £70.*

Consequently, Matt & Ronnie continue to shop with Tesco and have never had a problem since.

NB: In the interests of transparency, I feel it is important to concede that Matt did not resort to the Chinook in the end. The plan was set in motion and the logistics worked out but, before the rotors began turning, Matt found a local carpenter to work around the clock to build a new set. This is one of those occasions where a slight embellishment was acceptable. It didn't change the complaint but emphasized the ability to overcome a challenge.

Despite these obvious successes, it has not always been straightforward, and there have been a few occasions when no amount of time, effort or bleating will improve a dire situation. In those rare instances, your sanity rests on knowing when to stop, when to walk away and shrug the rage off, but I'll deal with that in Chapter 5, *Blood from Stones*.

In the meantime, there are other ways to achieve your goals. Sometimes you just need the right allies.

Chapter 4: Organ Grinders & Monkeys

You're ready to rage, your tongue has been sharpened, your pen is primed, the computer booted and you want justice, but do you know where your rage should be directed? How do you select your target?

Any company of a reasonable size will have a customer relations or customer services department. They no longer call them 'customer complaints' departments because that was altogether too negative and far too close to the truth for many of them. The customer relations departments are geared up for complaints. They are primed to deal with minor upsets and prepared to dilute the major issues. They exist to rebuild your trust in the company, to placate you when it has all become too much for you to deal with after a stressful week in the office, to listen, nod in agreement and fob you off with a platitude and a money-off voucher. Or, as is often the case, to absorb your complaint into the system, tell you it is being reviewed, file it in the shredder and then rely on you having a low boredom threshold and giving up.

To be fair, some companies do have particularly good customer relations departments, my favourite at the moment being Halfords. Mr. Kipling is also usually pretty good if you discover your French Fancies are crushed and their appearance spoiled your high tea with the vicar. Customer relations departments have their place and I'm not going to knock them too much. Companies set them up because they *want* you to write to them.

Let me clarify that. Companies don't *want* to receive a barrage of complaints, they simply want you to write to the customer relations department instead of anyone else within the company.

If you are narked because one of your eggs was cracked or the bottom Hobnob was mostly dust or you aren't very happy with the shape and texture of one of your cucumbers and all you want is a £2 voucher so that you can feel you got one over the big man, then customer services will do just fine. If you write a reasonably good letter they may even make it £5 AND you'll have already eaten the rest of the Hobnobs. Simple complaints often require only simple actions and receive (if you're lucky) simple responses. Sometimes. I'm still waiting for Somerfield to respond to my letter of 9th May 2006 about there being only five cookies in my bag of So Good Triple Chocolate Cookies instead of the usual six. It was one of those issues that wasn't worth pursuing after they ignored second letter. That, in Somerfield's case, is what the customer relations department is for.

If your complaint is more serious and hasn't merely narked you but has chipped the shiny coating off your day and you want to be taken seriously, don't contact customer relations.

Let me repeat that: *Don't* contact customer relations. Ignore them. If you are serious enough about complaining to be reading this book, that road is not for you. To steal a line from Sir Winston Churchill, *Never hold discussions with the monkey when the organ grinder is in the room.*

If your issue is serious enough for you to sit down with pen and paper or computer and invest an hour of your day composing an eloquent tirade to leave the recipient quivering in dread at the thought of ever meeting you, make sure it lands on the desk of the person or people whose day it will ruin most. The organ grinders are the people with the power and authority to act upon your complaint immediately and make your world sunny and bright again. They are also the men and women who care most about the damage you can do to them and their company.

Reputation matters to organ grinders. If you have a justifiable complaint that threatens their company's reputation, you also tarnish their personal reputation. Customer services staff generally don't care if the share price drops by ten points overnight; they will still have a job in the morning whether The Financial Times loves or hates the company. I'm not being flippant here; unless you're Erin Brockovich you are very unlikely to make a multi-national corporation crumble into dust and cause worldwide redundancies with your letter. The organ grinders on the other hand, well, a tarnished reputation and a drop in share price is a threat to their personal pride and their performance bonus. And that's *really* going to sting!

The organ grinders are the chairmen and women, the CEOs, COOs, the managing directors, the presidents and the owners. At a push feel free to lump in the vice-presidents, the executive vice-presidents and the board of directors. If they have leather-inlaid desks, buy books for their office by the metre, warrant an executive PA and have a Herman Miller chair around the vast, oval, oak table in the boardroom they are certainly worth considering as a target. The bigger the better.

Let's assume we're targeting a chairman. Chairman Bob of Great & Powerful Ltd. has just finished his telephone interview with Forbes and is preparing to slip out for a quick round of golf before his lunch meeting with the Secretary of State for Business, Innovation and Skills at Boodles when his executive PA knocks on the door and says, "I think you need to read this, Sir Bob..."

This is a letter stating that a kettle produced by Great & Powerful Ltd. has exploded taking most of a kitchen with it and singeing the eyebrows of Angry From Manchester's favourite (and currently, *only*) mother. Despite four letters to the customer relations department Angry has so far managed to secure only a standard letter that wasn't even signed, a voucher for £1.50 and the company's hopes that he will remain a loyal customer. Angry isn't best pleased and, as a matter of courtesy, is informing Sir Bob that he has an appointment with his solicitor this afternoon and an interview with BBC's *Watchdog* programme in the morning. Angry has concluded his letter with, *I am not at all at ease with my treatment at the hands of your despicable company, Sir Bob, and, with the help of my solicitor, the Great British press and my big, burly local MP, I am coming for you and a rather large slice of your eight-figure bonus. Have a nice day.*

I think we can quite safely assume that golf and lunch are off the agenda and Sir Bob's day has been severely stamped on. And if Sir Bob's day has been ruined, you can bet that he is about to find the subordinates responsible and ruin their day, too. Sir Bob is not used to receiving complaints. That's what his customer services department is for. So when such a letter somehow finds its way to his desk, it is a novelty and very, very concerning.

Most people complain to the monkeys because it doesn't dawn on them to approach anyone else. We are taught to do as we are told and convention tells us to complain to the right department. Well, (and if you are of a delicate disposition, cover your eyes for the rest of this sentence) bollocks to that!

Read the chapter heading again. Which one are you? Don't be the little guy, don't be another monkey. You, too, are an organ grinder so act like it! I give you permission to stop doing as you are told. Take a minute and listen to the Fraggles' song again. Grab that tail by the tiger! Go after the big cheeses; force them to meet you on equal terms. Don't bow, don't beg and don't scrape. Find the main man or woman and take him or her on. S/he may be titled and may earn seven figures more than you but you have justice on your side and little rocks can make great big ripples when thrown into the right spot of the pond.

It takes very little effort to find out who the big cheeses are, it just takes *some* effort and most people are lazy. Remember: Google is your friend! Usually the information will appear with a simple search of 'CEO of Great & Powerful Ltd.' but sometimes you may need to dig a little further. Most major companies will design their websites to reflect the products or service they provide and won't make it easy to navigate through to the company information you need. Look at the very bottom of the page, at the menu in the small print, for 'corporate', 'company information' or such like. Alternatively go back to Google and type in 'Great & Powerful board of directors.' If you try it with British Airways, for example, you will find a direct link to a page listing the entire management board that is a nightmare to find if you try going through the website's front door.

If that doesn't bear fruit, try a search on LinkedIn. It can be cumbersome if you have to search purely on the company name but I've stumbled upon some unlikely avenues that way. If all else fails try Companies House. For £1 per search you can dig up all sorts of information on every company listed in the UK, and £1 is an insignificant fee to pay if your reward is a new kitchen and a fresh set of eyebrows for your mum. Wikipedia (of course) has all manner of information but (of course) you need to take the information with a pinch of salt as it is written by ordinary folk and not Sir Bob himself. Another very useful resource is www.ceoemail.com, which does exactly what it says on the tin.

Double check everything before you write your letter. CEOs and chairmen/women move around from company to company and if you write to the wrong CEO you will immediately lose some of your credibility. Search for news stories in the broadsheets. Company big cheeses are rarely invisible and it should be easy enough to find a recent reference in one of the investment journals.

Why stop at one target? I have found on numerous occasions that a situation is resolved with more urgency if two or more organ grinders are targeted simultaneously. In such cases it is imperative that you make it very clear that you are writing to several people simultaneously, and who they are, for two reasons. Firstly, it is not fair to go behind your recipients' backs and to do so will be regarded as an underhand tactic. Secondly, you have the embarrassment factor. If the chairman knows the CEO has also received the letter there is no hiding from it. If they both know external organ grinders have also received the letter, they will be acutely aware that the situation is not as neatly contained as they would like it to be and will want to save face quickly.

In Chapter 5, *Blood from Stones,* I refer to a long and painful saga with the Department for Work and Pensions in which I initially targeted eight organ grinders, such was the appalling situation. When another corporate run-in hit crunch point, I eventually resorted to selecting about ten names from the board of directors and informed each of them that I would email them twice every day until one of them had the decency to deal with the issue. Unsurprisingly, on the afternoon of day two I received an email informing me that the situation had been resolved, my cheque was in the post and would I please regard the matter as closed and without need for further contact?

Mostly, however, one letter to one organ grinder is sufficient. Nutcrackers are necessary to open Brazil nuts, but peanuts are easily opened by hand. A sledgehammer in either case is going to leave you with very little to eat at the end of your attack on the shell.

Never underestimate the benefit of powerful friends. If you have a direct link to an organ grinder within the company or institution you are tackling, use them.

That link doesn't necessarily have to be a big cheese, either, just as long as s/he has the ear of a big cheese with the power and authority to deal with your case. When I trained at the Bristol Old Vic Theatre School, the principal was Chris Denys. I got on very well with him, I had personal dealings with him during my education there and after I had graduated, and he was the recognizable face and figurehead of the school. But the person who wielded the power and had the answer to every conceivable question, at least as far as we students were concerned, was Erika, the secretary!

When you complain, though you may address your letter to the CEO, more often than not the first response will come from his/her PA. S/he is the CEO's PA for a very good reason and, even if s/he is not always able to act on the CEO's behalf, they will have the very best and most direct line to the organ grinder. Respect the PA's position and your journey will be easier. Equally, I have crossed swords with more than one PA and in my work as a venue producer have battled with PAs over the tiniest of details only to discover that the person they assist is actually a thoroughly decent person. Be aware of them, respect them and understand the influence they quietly enjoy.

Having powerful friends on your side doesn't just mean knowing the right person in the company. Every single one of you is represented by a local MP, an MEP and a whole cabinet of ministers. On a smaller, more local level you also have parish and town councillors and you may even have a mayor. You may not have voted for any of them but they work for you. They are paid to represent you and your best interests. In effect, they are your servants, so use them.

It helps to know who your MP (and MEP, councillor, mayor etc.) is. If you don't, why not? I quite like to know who is playing with my money and deciding how they will next trash my road, village, country, planet... In Chapter 7, *The Complainer's Toolkit*, I have provided information to help you find cabinet members, MPs etc. It is far from an exhaustive list but it is a starting point for you.

Of course it helps to have a useful and respected MP but we're not all that fortunate. Growing up in Somerset my local MP was Paddy Ashdown. He had one of the safest seats in Parliament and was never threatened at election time because, quite frankly, he was fantastic. He knew his stuff, he cared about his work and he took very good care of his constituents. If we had a problem, Paddy Ashdown did his very best to take care of it and was usually very successful.

If you do have a great MP, you have a distinct advantage over many of us. If you don't, you could always move house, but that seems a little extreme. What you can do is train your MP, or at least push them in the direction you need them. Don't forget your MP is obliged to spend a certain amount of time holding surgeries for his/her constituents and must spend a portion of his/her time looking after the constituency and not purely devote his/her time to the Palace of Westminster.

Your MP is not only there for you in times of trouble. S/he is a very useful tool in times of public awareness, charitable promotion, school prize-giving, village fête opening and your exclusive point of contact if you would like tickets to Prime Minister's Question Time and a tour of the Palace of Westminster.

Although I mentioned the consideration of letters to multiple organ grinders, it does not count for MPs. You have *one* local MP and sending the identical letter to the other 649 (at time of writing) MPs is a pointless exercise. Not only are they tied up with the woes of their own constituents, they are also not permitted to interfere with other constituencies. Naturally, if you have an MP in the family, it can't hurt to try but that's nepotism and an entirely different matter.

You can, of course, write to the Prime Minister and/or the Deputy Prime Minister. It may raise your profile and there is an outside chance that one of them may even see your letter, but in my experience somebody will invariably reply on their behalf informing you that the PM/DPM was pleased to receive your letter, is unable to intervene personally and has passed your letter to the correct department. Where writing to the PM does help (beyond him being a family member) is when he is just one of the recipients and the other recipients are made aware that you are serious enough about your complaint to have involved Parliament.

If you have an issue that needs intervention at a governmental level, I would suggest you find the relevant department and write to the Secretary of State for that department. Again, I've provided assistance and links in Chapter 7, *The Complainer's Toolkit*, and in Chapter 5, *Blood from Stones*, I will outline the futility of involving the Department for Work and Pensions, high on my list of scoundrels.

A word of warning, though: As with any human resource, don't overuse your MP. Use every contact and resource sparingly and only when you really need them. Most of your complaints don't need the intervention of an MP and the more serious instances will usually be miraculously resolved by the mere threat of Parliament's involvement. Don't become the boy/girl who cried wolf or the dreaded constituent who bothers the MP weekly. I knew of a GP who had his own way of dealing with a hypochondriac who bothered him several times every month. He would pretend to listen and write notes while he doodled on his pad and would hand the hypochondriac a prescription for the cure-all wonder drug, ADT. However, his friend the pharmacist spilt the beans once. ADT stood for Any Damn Thing and generally took the form of the weakest Aspirin he had in stock. I'm sure your MP has similar ways of dealing with troublesome constituents.

The 'organ grinder' doesn't have to refer exclusively to the person to whom you write. Let's go back to the burger joint that served you up half a slug in your lunch. Many such fast food outlets are not branches of a large company but franchises, and so can be taken away from the proprietor. As I stated, your first choice for an effective complaint should be in person, immediately and to the person in charge. If the manager shrugs your complaint off and refuses to deal with it you are most likely to have success with the UK head office, if there is one. They will probably be responsible for the restaurant that you visited and most able to take swift action. Yes, the global head office is the organ grinder's organ grinder, but you may find that they are so far removed from the root of the problem that they ignore your complaint and hope you go away. Alternatively, they may send your letter or email back to the UK office, in which case you will have wasted time. If the issue is serious enough to be beyond the remit of the UK office, or they caused the problem in the first place, then go for it.

I had a glitch with Scandinavian Airlines (SAS) recently and, though they have a UK office, it felt foolish to deal with their subsidiary when the operation is run from Sweden. My thought was that the UK office didn't operate as a separate unit but as the local branch. In that instance I'm not sure if I made the wrong call or whether both offices would have passed the buck. SAS was only partially responsible for my delay (along with Heathrow Airport) and one of three companies involved in my being out of pocket. Though both SAS and Heathrow Airport passed the buck, First Great Western picked up the tab (**Case Study 3, Chapter 3**) so I felt no need to pursue it.

I've been promising to regale you with the story of the Utility Warehouse debacle for two chapters and it fits in with this chapter. As the letter below indicates, we were introduced to Utility Warehouse as a utilities broker that constantly seeks the cheapest utility suppliers and swaps the supplies accordingly with no inconvenience to the consumer. It's a fine idea. The sales rep, Ashley, raved about them and I have since met a couple of people who had a good experience with them. It was not the case for us.

My first approaches to Utility Warehouse were by telephone and to the customer services department. I've learned a great deal since then, and that, at least, is a positive outcome of this saga. Having worked my way through a number of telephone operatives whose names I failed to make note of during phone calls I failed to log, I insisted upon speaking with a manager and was presented with Nina. It was a most unpleasant interaction with a manager who had very little concept of customer care and even less desire to resolve the issue smoothly. It culminated in the following, lengthy letter to the chief executive and Otelo, the ombudsman. With hindsight and my experiences since, I would have written to The Honourable Charles Wigoder far earlier and proposed a swifter solution. However...

Case Study 7 – Utility Warehouse

This was a not my finest hour but it is worth including as a learning process. The telephone conversation with Sean/Shaun was so heated that, after he had shouted and sworn at me, I found myself standing at my desk and screaming down the phone at him, too. I have a feeling I also used one or two of the milder expletives in retaliation. I know for certain my wife closed two doors between us to try to escape and finally packed a flask of coffee and some cake and disappeared for several hours until I was calm again. It's not that I ignored my advice, I just hadn't learned enough to deal with an agonizing, horrible experience.

I should have insisted upon a manager immediately and when that had failed headed straight to the organ grinder at the very top.

Edward Field

13 January 2010

The Hon. Charles Wigoder, Chief Executive
Telecom *plus* PLC
Edge Business Centre
Humber Road
London
NW2 6EW

Dear Hon. Charles Wigoder

Re: Utility Warehouse account no. ████████

I wish to report and complain about the ineptitude, incompetence, poor customer service, inadequate communication, thoroughly offensive manner and the lies that I have suffered from Utility Warehouse. I have sent a copy of this letter to Otelo, the telecommunications Ombudsman.

My wife and I moved to the above address at the beginning of September 2009 from a house a few miles away in St. George, also in Bristol. After conversations with Ashley ████████, one of Utility Warehouse's representatives, we agreed to be supplied by the company with gas, electricity, a telephone line and broadband internet. I completed an application form on 14 September 2009 and sent it to Utility Warehouse. I would like to stress at this juncture that Ashley ████████ was entirely professional and attempted on numerous occasions to resolve the problems until he, too, was forced to lodge a complaint due to the embarrassment he suffered as a result of our appalling treatment.

There were issues with the gas and electricity supply but they were so minor in relation to the following issues that I will not waste your or my time by listing them here.

As far as I am concerned, the request was very simple: We required the Broadcall Plus service, which included the telephone line and broadband internet. We also requested to have our existing telephone number, 0117 ████████, transferred from our house in St. George to the current address. Both Ashley and the first representative I spoke to on the telephone agreed that this would be carried out.

In short, it wasn't. It appears that our supplier at the old address, Sky, failed to cancel our account fully and the telephone number was not released. Unfortunately, Utility Warehouse did not discover this at first and then failed to inform me why my application was continually rejected. It would appear that each time they attempted to book an installation for me, their system rejected it. On several occasions, the staff promised to phone me back when they had solved the problem. On every single occasion they failed to honour their promise.

When the promised engineers failed to materialize and no phone service was offered, I made a series of phone calls including the following:

7 October 2009 @ 15.54   19 October 2009 @ 19.19

20 October 2009 @ 8.43   20 October 2009 @ 9.52

22 October 2009 @ 12.44

On each occasion the staff failed to call me back with a solution or further information. As I am sure you will understand, I was frustrated and felt severely let down by Utility Warehouse by this stage and was only appeased when a telephone operative promised that a manager would call me to resolve the situation within 48 hours. Needless to say, none did!

On 27 October 2009 at 11.19 I phoned yet again and spoke at length with an operative named Sean/Shaun. I would request that you listen to this phone call in its entirety as I believe it was recorded and will support my letter. Sean became incredibly insulting and would not listen to me. Regardless of the number of times I tried to explain the situation, he insisted that he was looking at my application form and that I had completed it incorrectly. He insulted me and shouted, stating that it was not his fault that I could not complete a form properly and I should just accept that I had given the wrong information. I tried in vain to tell him that I was also looking at my copy of the form and that the information was entirely correct according to what the form requested i.e. in the heading 'Supply address' I entered the address to be supplied: ███████████. In the heading 'Phone number to be connected to this service' I listed the number that I wished to be connected: 0117 ███████.' As I stated repeatedly to Sean, even while he was shouting at me, I know where I live. I do know my address and phone number and had listed them absolutely correctly. I have my copy of the form if you wish to see it.

Sean also claimed that the promised phone call within 48 hours *had* been made to me. I checked my mobile phone records and informed him that, despite his insistence, no phone calls were received or missed from Utility Warehouse's number (which he confirmed was 0844 8157777), according to my phone's log. He then stated that he was checking the notes on my file as we spoke and that they stated clearly that a phone call had been made to me within 48 hours to 0117 ███████ i.e. the phone number that I do not have because they had failed to transfer it and, even if they had, I would have been unable to receive it because I did not have a telephone line to connect my phone to because Utility Warehouse had still not sent out an engineer!!!

Sean then promised that a manager, Nina, would call me within the hour. Unfortunately, I missed the call and so at 13.51 I called her back. I informed Nina of what Sean had said and she contradicted him. She stated quite categorically that there was no record of which phone number the promised phone call had been made to. Either Sean or Nina lied to me. Again, please listen to this phone call as it, too, was recorded. I attempted to explain the situation again and Nina also refused to accept that Utility Warehouse had made a mistake. You will hear in the recording that voices again were raised and that Nina curtly stated that I should accept that it was "pretty stupid of me to fill in the wrong address." She was incredibly patronizing and insulting and again refused to listen. Eventually she read the form properly and realized that *she* and Utility Warehouse had made the mistake and not me. She agreed to cancel the contract without any charges whatsoever.

However, on 30 November 2009, my bank account was debited by £87.13: a payment to Utility Warehouse. Whilst I am happy to pay for all gas and electricity that I used, I refuse to pay the portion of this that was for Broadcall during November because British Telecom have supplied me with a phone line and broadband since 20 October 2009! They also managed to do so within 24 hours.

On 12 January 2010 I received several emails from Utility Warehouse informing me that my next bill was available. I was not able to open then and I do not accept that I should receive any bills after Nina's assurances and so, at 16.45 I phoned Utility Warehouse again. The operative was only able to confirm that I had been charged for Broadcall despite *never* having received *any* aspect of the service and so he assured me that Nina would call me as soon as possible to resolve the issue.

Today, at 12.36, Nina did indeed phone me. She was once again abrasive, curt and condescending and refused to listen to me properly. She again claimed that it was just my point of view, and not a matter of fact as my records and the recorded telephone conversation prove conclusively, and that she disagreed with it. She did say that she would refund the money in February but I was unable to confirm how much or request written confirmation because she again refused to listen, talked over me and abruptly ended the conversation with 'Thank you and goodbye' and promptly hung up on me.

I still don't have any assurance that this debacle will be finally resolved and that Utility Warehouse will refrain from contacting me ever again, that I will receive a full refund and will not be charged a single penny for the services that I have *never* received or benefited from.

Additionally, until BT installed my phone line I was forced to make all of my calls to Utility Warehouse on the premium line number for which I was charged 25 pence per minute. My O2 phone bill has jumped dramatically and I estimate that Utility Warehouse has cost me about £50 in phone calls alone.

On top of this I have been insulted, shouted at and lied to repeatedly. I fail to understand when or where there is ever a situation when any of this gross incompetence or thoroughly insulting and offensive behaviour is tolerable or remotely acceptable. How can you possibly justify running a company this way?

I look forward to your response and details of how you will resolve this issue.

Yours faithfully

Edward Field.

Success rating: 4/10 – In frustration and a desire to eradicate Utility Warehouse from my mind, I shredded every letter I received from Utility Warehouse and I cannot recall the exact outcome. I know that eventually all bills were cancelled and I didn't pay a single penny of the charges but my telephone expenses for calls to their premium number from my mobile were not reimbursed and I did not receive any compensation of any form. Even now when I see the Utility Warehouse logo I shudder and nothing could ever induce me to use them again. If Utility Warehouse was the last supplier left on earth I would cook over a flame, wash in a river and communicate by smoke signal. A horrible, horrible experience.

By 2013 I had an array of very successful complaints to add to my pile of painful, failed, 'learning experiences' and had undertaken complaints for various friends and family members. I don't think it's that more bad things happen to me, it is more a case that I now see the opportunity for justice and recompense where others choose to privately moan about it or decide it isn't worth bothering about. I find a definite pleasure in righting wrongs for myself and others and believe strongly that if we don't take responsibility for highlighting injustice, shoddy workmanship and poor service, how can the perpetrators be forced to take responsibility for putting it right?

Yes, mistakes happen despite the best efforts and the most professional and thoughtful attitudes. That is not the problem. My gripe, and the reason I happily grind my axe to its sharpest edge, is with people and institutions that don't care and don't make the requisite efforts to put things right when mistakes occur. Cineworld Cinemas is one such institution that irks me and warrants a letter every couple of years.

When Cineworld introduced its Unlimited card, I quietly cheered. Films are one of my passions. Even before I began reviewing new releases on my website, The Squiss, I used to clock up far more film viewings than the average cinemagoer and it was an expensive hobby. Now I average ten films per month, 120 per year, and with my Unlimited card, as long as I see at least three films per month, I'm in credit. But saving me money does not excuse Cineworld or anyone else from their responsibilities. The fact is, if I am paying for a product or service that you don't provide in accordance with your own claims and promises then, as my mother used to proclaim before waving the potato masher, *Woe betide you...*

Inexperience led me to address my first Cineworld letter from 2007 to the 'Customer Care Department' and, understandably, it was ignored. By the time I wrote this one to the chairman, however, I had learned much and won frequently.

Case Study 8 – Cineworld Cinemas

This one had been brewing for a while. I had attempted to resolve the situation on the telephone and by letter with those directly responsible for the Unlimited cards but they had failed repeatedly to find a solution and so I sought the organ grinder.

Squircle Entertainment

Not quite a square; not quite a circle...

edward@squircleentertainment.com   www.squircleentertainment.com   www.squiss.co.uk
Squircle Entertainment,
+44 (0)   Twitter: @edwardsquircle

9 January 2013

Mr. Anthony Herbert Bloom, Chairman
Cineworld Group PLC
Power Road Studios
114, Power Road
London
W4 5PY

Dear Mr. Bloom

Being a frequent Cineworld customer and an Unlimited card holder for more than six years, I can understand entirely why the company you preside over would choose to consistently ignore me. Why should Cineworld possibly care about someone who hands over their money every month and patronizes your establishments approximately 100 times per year (see www.squiss.co.uk for further details)?

However, I'm not going away and I will continue to write, email, phone and complain until somebody has the courtesy to respond and deal with the issues.

Further to my previous contact via email and phone, my wife and I have still not received our upgraded black cards. I have listened to the long recorded message on the Unlimited Helpdesk (0844 3723 445) that very unhelpfully cuts one off without an option to speak to a human being. We have not moved house or changed our address or any other details for over a year and I know Cineworld has our current address (   ) because somebody on the customer services team acknowledged my change of address letter in the autumn of 2011. Back in November I was assured that our cards would arrive by mid December. A month later we are still waiting.

Please will you arrange for the replacement cards to be sent, please, as your staff seems incapable or unwilling? Our card details, once again, are as follows:

Marieke Field 633577   Edward Field 633577

Further more, we *still* do not receive email notification of Unlimited screenings. As I detailed at length in correspondence with your customer services team in November, I have checked and rechecked my account settings on the Cineworld site to ensure I receive emails but the only emails I receive are the standard weekly emails detailing the films and screening times.

It is becoming increasingly frustrating dealing with Cineworld, and the staff at the cinema groan in agreement every time they ask why we *still* do not have our cards and I am forced to explain again. When your customers are frustrated at your ineptitude and your staff members shrug because they are acutely aware of Cineworld's lack of customer care, it is an indication that you have a serious issue.

On a sideline issue, I think eight months (approximately) is more than sufficient for the absence of soap dispensers in the men's toilets to have been noticed as, presumably, the toilets are cleaned throughout the day and frequent requests have been made to reinstate them.

I look forward to your response.

Yours sincerely

Edward Field.

Success rating: 7/10 – I received a superb email from Mr. Bloom just a few days later apologizing profusely, promising to instruct his staff to resolve the issue immediately and complimenting the reviews on my website. There was no gift or compensation, but that wasn't something I was particularly concerned about, and within a week our cards had arrived and everything was perfect in Cineworld. Until the next occasion.

Armed with reason, understanding, determination and the right contact I have found it is usually possible to make an effective complaint that is resolved swiftly and consigned to memory while a pleasant feeling warms the body and a gift of compensation makes the day bright and sparkly again. But every now and again one stumbles across a stubborn beast that raises the blood pressure, elevates its middle finger and absolutely will not yield.

Chapter 5: Blood from Stones

I struggled with the title for this chapter. Initially it was *Unwinnable Causes*. Then *Unwinnable Causes & Last Resorts*. It was even briefly *Calling on St. Jude,* Saint Jude being the Roman Catholic patron saint of desperate cases and lost causes. Finally, adapting one of many suggestions offered by my friend and fellow writer, Ben Mears (The *Tyler May* series of books), I selected a title that reflects the effort and futility of some of my campaigns to date.

There have been occasions where, though an occurrence or transaction has twanged my sense of justice, I have inhaled, counted to ten, exhaled and moved on. Sometimes my workload has been so extreme that, though I really shouldn't have found a bite mark on my bar of chocolate, it has been too much effort and too much of a drain on my limited time to follow it up. There are plenty of occasions where, on a sliding scale of 0-10, the injustice has barely passed 2 and, besides, there is tennis on the box.

There have even been one or two situations where the behemoth that has wronged me is untouchable and the consequences of attempting an assault on their misdemeanour would far exceed the initial frustration. In my limited experience, dalliances with the Avon and Somerset Constabulary fall into this last category. Don't get too excited; a couple of bog-standard speeding tickets aside, I am a thoroughly boring individual when it comes to unlawful activities. Drunken pranks in student days were either overlooked or settled with a slap on the wrist and even if I had committed any more serious crimes since, I clearly haven't been caught and wouldn't be so foolish as to highlight them here.

Two clashes with my local police force *do* warrant a mention, if only as examples of when not to rock the boat:

In 1996, in my first year at the Bristol Old Vic Theatre School, one of my many jobs required a late night walk home from Clifton Village to Henleaze. On one such walk home with a colleague, we realised we were being followed, slowly, by a police car. The car matched our speed until, running out of road, the cops decided to block our path and stop us. Two officers, one male, one female, climbed out of the car. To her credit, the policewoman did at least have the good grace to appear embarrassed by what happened next. Her male colleague pushed me against the wall, dropped my bag on the ground and frisked me roughly. When he had finished, I asked him, what I had done wrong and why he had searched me.

He sneered at me, "You have long hair, a leather jacket and a rucksack. What other reason do I need?"

It annoyed me at the time and perhaps I should have taken the matter further, but my feeling was that it was his word against mine and who would believe a young student over a police officer? I also believe that, ultimately, bullies do get their comeuppance. Perhaps some time later he pushed the wrong person too far...

*

The second notable occurrence took place a few months later. We were in production at the Theatre Royal and I was on my way home, just the right side of midnight and almost at the end of Clifton Downs, barely five minutes from my front door. An unmarked car sped past me, braked suddenly, accelerated, did a U-turn into a side street up ahead and stopped, the occupants obviously watching me as I approached.

I assumed they were probably cops, the alternative being rather more unpleasant and not worth dwelling on, glared at them and continued walking. Moments later I realised a helicopter overhead was tracking me. Then the blue flashing lights caught up with me, a police car screeched to a halt in front of me and two more cops climbed out.

The first of them demanded to know who I was, why I was out late at night on my own and where I was going. He made no attempt to disguise his obvious mistrust of me and when I asked him why I had been stopped again he responded, "Someone matching your exact description has just been reported for stealing a car and joyriding."

I smiled at him with as much contempt as I could muster, held his stare and coldly stated, "I'm *walking!*"

There seemed little point in taking the matter further. Stupidity is not a crime and I was left with an anecdote to dine out on for evermore.

Mostly, though, a wrongdoing is not only worth challenging, it is important to challenge it, lest the perpetrators think they can continue to escape justice. Usually, as I have attested, it is straightforward or a minor skirmish until David triumphs over Goliath, but sometimes a complaint demands more effort, more determination and a decision to fight to the metaphorical death.

Alas, in the course of one or two such battles that I was convinced I would win because logic, reason and justice were so clearly in my corner, I was forced to limp away, battle-scarred, bloody of nose and tail between my legs. I don't regret my decision to head into battle with them, but I would give you the benefit of my unpleasant experiences and advise you to either back away or learn from my mess and avoid a situation requiring a confrontation in the first place.

It is difficult not to regard miscarriages of justice as a personal failure and one can be left reeling or fuming at the absolute refusal of someone to take responsibility and make amends, even when the law is an absolute ass, but sometimes you just have to know when to quit.

When it came to the Department for Work and Pensions (DWP) it was a lengthy battle. I remain convinced I was shafted and it still rankles, but after six months of arguing, reasoning, pleading and battling, I finally closed the drawer on my filing cabinet and walked away.

A little background information is called for first. Though I trained as a stage manager and pay the rent largely through related work in the events industry, the scales are slowly tipping towards more writing and live voice work, but when employment in my chosen fields is in short supply, particularly in the summer months, I fall back on decorating as I have done for many years. The manual work has unfortunately broken me. My shoulders click and cause me to wince after a day of sanding or rolling, and drilling through rock and masonry has left me with tennis elbow in both arms, the left arm due to over compensating for the pain and restricted use of the right.

After years of physiotherapy, ultrasound treatment and even steroid injections, my GP gave up and sent me for surgery. It is a relatively simple operation, performed under a general anaesthetic, which renders one's arm useless for several weeks. Complete rest is required for the arm, followed by exercises and more physiotherapy until the arm is strong enough to manage light tasks. When one is right-handed and depends on the right arm for shaving, eating and for every avenue of employment, the temporary loss of the arm makes paying the rent something of a challenge.

Initially, my GP signed me off work for six weeks. I received incapacity benefit and the immediate future was provided for. At the end of the six weeks, though I was able to drive and take on voice work or writing jobs, traditionally the summer offers little. 2012 was no different and my usual back up plan of manual work was out of the question.

Reluctantly, I telephoned the Job Centre, completed all the necessary forms over the phone and, dispensing with my pride, applied for Jobseekers Allowance (JSA), Housing Benefit and a temporary exemption from paying Council Tax. It was an inauspicious experience from the beginning as it transpires there are two forms of JSA: income-based and contributions-based. In my ignorance I enquired which one I should apply for.

"I can't tell you that. That's up to you."

"But I don't know which one is relevant to me. What happens if I pick the wrong one?"

"It will be rejected."

"If you were in my position, which one would you apply for?"

"I can't tell you that. That's up to you."

Decision made (I still don't know if it was the best one for me), the lady booked an appointment for me with the Job Centre in Bath, reminding me to take the required proof of identification. Having copies of my passport on file, I decided to save the government money and took one of them with me, ensuring I had my actual passport, too, as I expected them to request to see it in the flesh.

They did, and then the administrator said she needed to make a copy. I proffered my copy, explained about saving money and resources only to be informed that a photocopy wasn't acceptable. The presence of my actual passport in her hand did nothing to convince her that the image on the sheet of paper in my hand was exactly what her photocopier would produce.

"It doesn't count if I don't copy it!"

Without need to exaggerate, I assure you I stood and watched for a good six minutes as she attempted repeatedly to photocopy my passport onto a single sheet of A4 paper. Sheet after sheet of A3 emerged with complete, partial and enlarged copies. After about eight had emerged, been screwed up and thrown into the bin in disgust, she asked a colleague to help and together they repeated the process, utilizing both the A3 and A4 feed trays. After the eighteenth or nineteenth attempt, she returned to her desk with a single copy.

Apparently the correct response is not, "Wow! That looks *exactly* like my copy."

I was eventually awarded JSA and Housing and Council Tax Benefit. Or so I thought. I knew there would be a delay in receiving my JSA and so I didn't query it but concentrated on finding work so that I could escape the benefits black hole as quickly as possible. I don't wish to discredit or belittle those who genuinely need benefits, but it was not a road I wished to travel for a day longer than absolutely necessary. Rather than recount every detail, I'll lay out a few of the many letters I wrote between November 2012 and February 2013 when it became clear that 'the system' was very much against me.

Case Study 9a – Department for Work & Pensions

At the time of writing this letter I was frustrated and felt helpless. My claim had been rejected, the rent was due, accounts were drained and answers not forthcoming from the various departments of the DWP, namely the Job Centre Plus etc. My letters had been ignored and my phone calls unanswered. I was discovering a culture of passing the buck within the department and I was rapidly believing my naïvety, ignorance of the system and honesty were having unfortunate repercussions.

However, I followed my rules of openness with multiple recipients, continued honesty, a firm statement of my case and a request for a swift resolution.

Squircle Entertainment

Not quite a square; not quite a circle...

edward@squircleentertainment.com   www.squircleentertainment.com   www.squiss.co.uk
Squircle Entertainment,
+44 (0)█████████   Twitter: @edwardsquircle

28 November 2012

CC to:

Rt Hon Iain Duncan Smith MP, Secretary of State for Work and Pensions, Caxton House, Tothill Street, London, SW1H 9DA

Jacob Rees-Mogg MP, House of Commons, London SW1A 0AA

Nick █████, Job Centre Plus District Manager, ████████████████████

Lynda ████, Group Partnership Manager, ████████████████████

Paula █████, Manager, ██████████████████████████████

Mr. Nick ████████

Dear Mr. Nick ████████

Reference: National Insurance no. ████████
Housing/Council Tax Benefit Claim Ref: ████████
Council Tax Reference: ████████

In the interest of transparency and honesty, I would like to draw your attention to the fact that I have also sent this letter to the addressees listed above, as I have faced such a wall of bureaucracy and ill-treatment with numerous instances of Job Centre staff 'passing the buck', that I no longer know who has the authority, ability or interest to help me. Consequently, I have selected the five people I feel may, or should, be in a position to resolve this issue.

I apologise that this is such a long letter and detailed saga for you to digest but, in my defence, you are requested to read it *once* whilst I have recounted this matter on more occasions than I can genuinely remember and have fought it over several weeks. Please bear with me and I shall offer as much detail as I can so that you may understand the situation fully.

I became a sole trader in September 2002 and, in order to work as much and as often as possible to support my wife and myself, I have undertaken freelance contracts over the past decade as writer (scripts, copy, journalism, speeches, reviews etc.), stage management (corporate parties, award ceremonies, rock concerts etc.), venue production (conferences, world congresses), event creation (bespoke quizzes, treasure hunts, Generation Game-themed events), director/casting director (corporate videos), voice over/voice of god (award ceremonies, corporate events), set building and, when work is in short supply (as with the current economic climate), I have turned to painting and decorating in order to pay the rent.

In my event management and production work to date I have worked with VIPs including President Clinton, HRH Prince Andrew, Prime Minister the Rt Hon Tony Blair, First Minister of Scotland Alex Salmond, H.E. Wen Jiabao, H.E Ban Ki-moon, Hans-Jorgen Koch, Lord Norman Foster and royalty, dignitaries and ministers from across Europe, Asia and the Middle East. I have venue produced or stage managed the likes of The Word Future Energy Summit, Gastech, ADIPEC, GlaxoSmithKline, The English National Ballet, Scouting for Girls, Alexandra Burke and Ed Sheeran and written award ceremony scripts for presenters such as Chris Barrie, Rufus Hound, Rhod Gilbert and Hugh Dennis.

I have shaken hands with presidents one day and then scraped mould of bathroom walls the next as I return to decorating.

I don't mention this out of need for appreciation but simply to make it clear that I work when I can, I am not a habitual claimant and I am *very* uncomfortable about 'sponging' from the state. My CVs, that you will find on my websites attest to the variety and status of my work and any records you still hold for me will indicate that the last time I claimed income assistance from the state was almost twenty years ago before I retrained as a stage manager. My unfortunate need to seek temporary financial aid is, as my file will show, purely down to an injury sustained at work and subsequent surgery for lateral epicondylitis.

My need to claim financial support is in no way due to a reluctance to work, rather an *inability* to work for a period of months and, subsequently, a lack of work due to the current economic climate and my being 'out of the system', a situation I am remedying as my recent short contracts suggest.

On 20th June 2012 I attended the Royal United Hospital in Bath for surgery to resolve my on-going problems with tennis elbow. I was signed off by my GP until the end of September and I received Employment and Support Allowance (ESA). Although I have been advised my arm may take up to a year to heal fully, I felt able to use it and seek work at the beginning of October. As I had not secured any work and wanted to be completely honest, I contacted Job Centre Plus via the St Austell Benefit Centre, the address and contact number listed on all correspondence I have received regarding my claim, regarding my situation and was advised that my ESA would cease and as of 4th October 2012 I would receive Jobseekers Allowance (JSA).

I gave all the details of my claim over the phone and then attended Bath Job Centre for meetings with claims staff. Over the course of almost two hours, I completed a series of forms providing identical information to two different people working for the same department because, apparently, no claim information is stored or made available to other staff using the network when claims are transferred or amended.

In each case I made exactly the same statement about my operation, my desire to work, my availability to work, my status as a sole-trader, the many and various types of work I am able to undertake and my willingness to accept full-time employment if it became available. The gentleman in Bath, whose name eludes me but was to be my signing officer, made it very clear that he didn't expect to see me for very long based on the effort I was demonstrating in my search for work, my skills, my multiple trades, my positive outlook and they way I exceeded all requirements.

I am sure that if you contact him he will recall our long conversation as we discussed the arts, travel and my work and he seemed genuinely interested in my work as I was such a 'novelty' in his experience at the Job Centre. I had previously signed a contract of sorts in which I was required to provide evidence of a specific quantity of phone calls, emails, on-line searches and other endeavours to secure employment. He was vocally surprised when I handed him the logbook and he stated that some claimants struggle to complete a single page between signing dates whilst I had filled the entire booklet in just one week.

If you take the time to read my file, you should see, and I am confident he will confirm, that I am willing to work eighteen hours per day seven days per week and am available for work twenty four hours a day anywhere across the globe. In the events industry I have become used to working excessive hours. Indeed, as a driver, set-builder and stage manager on award ceremonies I regularly worked twenty-seven hour shifts. My statements were repeatedly clear: I am willing and able to work and will consider anything within the arenas of event management, production, writing, voiceovers and decorating.

However, it would appear this is not sufficient.

I have not received a single JSA payment and have received no financial support from Job Centre Plus since the final payment of ESA on 3rd October 2012. Despite repeated phone calls I received little information and no practical assistance. I have continued my search for work and have been 'penciled' on six VOG jobs through October and November only to see my role cut due to the clients' budget reductions.

I was then offered a VOG for the ▆▆▆▆▆▆▆ Awards on ▆▆▆▆▆▆ November 2012 at the Sheraton Park Lane and I duly phoned Job Centre Plus to inform them that I wished to sign off as of that date. The lady I spoke with urged me not to sign off as it was for just one day but my hope was that it would lead to more work fairly quickly and the income from it would certainly exceed the weekly limit. The lady said my outstanding and unresolved claim for JSA would not be affected and I would receive all benefit owing to me. She provided me with another number to call for an update on my claim.

My log of these calls includes the following:

1. Monday 12th November – called at 9.00am. Promised a call back.
2. Monday 12th November – no call back received by 4.30pm.
3. Monday 12th November – still no call back received. Phoned again 5.15pm.
4. Monday 12th November – informed my case was sent to a 'decision maker' on Thursday. I will receive a call back between 9.00 and 10.00 tomorrow.
5. Tuesday 13th November – no call back received. Phoned again 10.08.
6. Tuesday 13th November – not sure what was resolved. Transferred to automated department to reset PIN before she explained. Try calling again at 3.00
7. Tuesday 13th November - received a phone call at 11.48. Claim will be closed as of 15th November. Everything will be settled by mid-week next week (21st) and outstanding payments made.

However, on the afternoon of 14th November, my client called me to apologise that they had booked two VOGs and so I was no longer required. I phoned various departments including Job Centre Plus to let them know the situation and my claim was extended for another week as I had a further VOG booked for ▆▆▆▆▆▆ November for the ▆▆▆▆▆▆▆▆ Awards at the Grange Tower Bridge Hotel. They requested I drive to Bath to sign on late as that would have been my signing day had I not signed off. I happily obliged and the lady I saw on the ground floor sympathized with my predicament and assured me that she had made comprehensive notes to support my statement and that my claim would indeed be extended until 22nd November.

So as not to go through the same situation again, I phoned up to sign off again on Friday 23rd November:

1. Friday 23rd November – Phoned up to sign off again. 13.21. Informed that I cannot sign off as I'm not signing on. My claim has apparently been closed! Cut off.
2. Friday 23rd November – Phoned again, cut off again.
3. Friday 23rd November – Phoned again. Transferred to wrong job centre this time!
4. Friday 23rd November – Another attempt. 14.20. Explained situation in detail to the lady. Transferred. Informed my claim has been rejected because I am apparently in full-time employment. Tried to explain and requested she read my file completely. She informed me that because I am self-employed I am regarded as being in full-time employment and have stated I am not fully available for work! She would not listen to reason. Said to wait for the letter and appeal.

On Saturday 24th November I received a letter dated 21st November stating:

We cannot pay you an allowance from 22 October 2012. This is because: you are working for 16 hours or more per week.

I am not sure why that date was given as my claim is from 4th October 2012.

It is now 28th November 2012 and I have not received any payments from Job Centre Plus since 3rd October 2012. I have another VOG booked for tomorrow, 29th November but my invoice for this and last week's VOG will not be paid for about six weeks. I am also providing relief cover as Front of House manager at the Tobacco Factory Theatre in Bristol but generally for just two or three shifts per week of between four and six hours at a rate of just £⬛ per hour.

Please will you tell me how to pay the rent and bills and how to buy food? Please will you tell me how to pay for the fuel to drive to work?

I don't want to sign on. I don't wish to claim from the state and I am hopeful that very soon work will come in. Besides, it's just too hard to deal with Job Centre Plus and the related departments.

If you take the time to contact those who have directly spoken with me in Bath, they will confirm that I have not been working, I have repeatedly expressed an immense desire to work, I have stated repeatedly that I will work wherever and whenever work is available, though I am registered as a sole trader I have not been working and I fail to understand how my lack of employment and absolute willingness to work can be confused with full-time employment and unavailability for work.

I am writing to you all because I have to take this personally. It surely has to be a personal attack because if this was the norm the press would be filled with such stories. Please would somebody be kind enough to explain why my honesty with the various governmental departments and willingness to work has placed me in a very precarious financial position? On reflection and based on what I see around me and what others report, my best chance of support is to lie and cheat the system. Unfortunately I was brought up to listen to my conscience.

I'm not interested in a flash car, in a widescreen TV, in a holiday, in a council house, in a complete Sky package. I would just like to pay the bills and for my wife and I to eat every day. I am very hopeful that in the new year work will come in. If reason is seen and my claim is approved, the outstanding balance may just about get us through to January when the VOG invoices will be paid.

If that is not possible, please will you offer a practical solution? After much deliberation, other than a distasteful approach to a tabloid, I can find only one alternative to recoup the income we were relying on but have lost. This is to invoice Job Centre Plus for my time and fuel to attend pointless meetings, complete ignored documents and forms, provide countless explanations and write numerous applications and letters at an acceptable rate for a writer, VOG or venue producer. By charging each interaction on a minimum half-day rate at £⬛ per day (a very low rate if you look at what top VOGs like ⬛ or writers such as ⬛ charge) by my reckoning I can invoice Job Centre Plus for £⬛ give or take.

Please will you take the time to make some calls, read my file and see reason? I don't want much, I'd just like to receive what I was told I was entitled to so that it sees us through to my first payment for honest employment.

Yours sincerely

Edward Field.

Success rating: 2/10 – As expected, I received the standard letter from Ian Duncan Smith's assistant informing me my letter had been passed along, Anonymous 'on behalf of Lynda ⬛ informed me my letter had been passed to the Customer Resolutions Team, Jacob Rees-Mogg wrote to say he was looking into it and I have no record of a personal response from either Nick ▮▮▮▮ or Paula ▮▮▮▮

Case Study 9b – Department for Work & Pensions

After various telephone calls, I was informed my case had been forwarded to a 'decision maker'. I was given a new contact, Judith ▮▮▮▮ Complaints Resolution Manager, who later informed me that the decision maker had again rejected my claim because I was apparently employed for fifty hours per week and therefore not entitled to benefit. Again, my honesty had got me into trouble and so I wrote to the nameless, faceless decision maker.

Squircle Entertainment

Not quite a square; not quite a circle...

edward@squircleentertainment.com www.squircleentertainment.com www.squiss.co.uk
Squircle Entertainment,
+44 (0)   Twitter: @edwardsquircle

22 December 2012

The Decision Maker
Bath Job Centre

Dear Decision Maker

Reference: National Insurance no.
Housing/Council Tax Benefit Claim Ref:
Council Tax Reference:

Further to my lengthy letter of 23 November 2012 and subsequent phone call and letter from your colleague, Judith ▮▮▮▮, which I received today, I request that you reconsider my claim that you previously rejected. The reason that you apparently rejected my claim was that I was supposedly working full time and therefore unable to undertake any further paid employment. This is not true, as I have stated repeatedly.

The figure of fifty hours has been mentioned as the total number of hours I have allegedly been working while claiming (unpaid) benefits. Please understand, I have not been employed for such hours.

When I was employed I regularly worked such hours, for example, when I was driving, building sets and stage managing award ceremonies, such jobs would be 27 hours in length. The working day in the events industry is substantially longer than most factory workers, shop workers of civil servants etc. and on a conference I regularly still work fourteen hours per day. When not actually on a job, I would also need to undertake 'work' (i.e. *not* employment) at home such as emails, research, preparation and script editing etc. in order to make my life a great deal easier on site and to enable the job to run smoothly.

Once my benefit had been changed to Job Seekers' Allowance because I was healthy enough to work, I worked at home in an attempt to generate employment. I was required by the Job Centre to demonstrate that I was seeking work and not simply sponging from the welfare state and when I was asked how many hours I was prepared to put in, I plucked an arbitrary figure out of the air of fifty hours. As I stated in my previous letter, the gentleman at the Bath Job Centre was amazed that I was putting in so much work in order to generate employment. I cannot be certain how much work I did put in and there is every chance that it wasn't as much as fifty hours but I was, and remain, determined to find employment and that is not achieved by sitting at home watching TV or reading; it is achieved by online research, writing letters, sending out CVs, arranging and attending meetings, writing prospective pitches and articles. I respectfully ask you to understand the difference between my 'work' during this period and 'employment'.

I find it utterly absurd that I am being penalized for my endeavours to find work and understand I would have been far better off doing the bare minimum. However, that is not the work ethic instilled in me. I find it also very concerning that you made such a harsh decision, based on a misunderstanding, according to Judith ████████, and didn't think to pick up the phone and ask me. I would happily have met with you, explained everything and avoided many, many weeks of frustration and financial hardship.

In case there is still any misunderstanding, please understand I was not employed, but I put in a great deal of effort to gain employment.

I sincerely hope you will see reason this time. I hope you will also understand my need to take this as far as necessary to resolve this and so will be contacting all of the addressees on my previous letter if I do not hear favourably from you by return post.

Yours sincerely

Edward Field.

Success rating: 0/10 – I waited, I phoned, I waited, I phoned again, I argued. Judith informed me my case had not been marked as urgent despite her promise it would be, and ultimately the decision maker, now given a name, decided to uphold her decision because, apparently, the law states that I was working and therefore not available for work. The requirements for JSA also state I must show evidence of my efforts to seek work. It was abundantly clear, even to Judith, that I had exceeded my obligations and she could see that I had not earned any money from my effort to find employment. My note for the phone conversation with Judith on 17th January 2013 at 9.45 reads simply: Judith called back. "Nothing I can do."

Case Study 9c – Department for Work & Pensions

I wrote the following letter immediately to Judith and sent copies to seven people aware of my case, including the Deputy Prime Minister, Nick Clegg (with the predictable result), the Prime Minister, David Cameron (also with the predictable result), Ian Duncan Smith (ditto), and my local MP, Jacob Rees-Mogg.

My tone changed and I resorted to angry cynicism. I think by this stage I had virtually given up all hope but there was still a part of me that thought How dare they!

Squircle Entertainment ℭ

Not quite a square; not quite a circle...

---

edward@squircleentertainment.com   www.squircleentertainment.com   www.squiss.co.uk
Squircle Entertainment,
+44 (0) ▮▮▮   Twitter: @edwardsquircle

17 January 2013

Judith ▮▮▮
Complaints Resolution Manager
▮▮▮▮▮▮▮▮

CC to:

Rt Hon David Cameron MP, 10 Downing Street, London, SW1A 2AA

Rt Hon Nick Clegg MP, 70 Whitehall, London, SW1A 2AS

Rt Hon Iain Duncan Smith MP, Secretary of State for Work and Pensions, Caxton House, Tothill Street, London, SW1H 9DA

Jacob Rees-Mogg MP, House of Commons, London SW1A 0AA

Nick ▮▮▮, Job Centre Plus District Manager ▮▮▮▮▮▮

Lynda ▮▮▮, Group Partnership Manager, ▮▮▮▮▮

Paula ▮▮▮, Manager, ▮▮▮▮▮

Dear Ms. Judith ▮▮▮

Reference: National Insurance no. ▮▮▮
Housing/Council Tax Benefit Claim Ref: ▮▮▮
Council Tax Reference: ▮▮▮

As with my letter of 23 November 2012, I would like to draw your attention to the fact that I have also sent this letter to the addressees listed above. I realise that some of the addressees ignored me, that some said they cannot help and that some said they would 'look into the situation' but every single one of you has failed to resolve this and so I am forced to write again. In desperation, you will note that I have included two more names to the list.

If any of you care to meet with me, I will explain in detail and show you all the letters and logged phone calls so that you understand the situation fully. In the meantime, I have enclosed a letter dated 20th December 2012 from Judith ▮▮▮ and my reply dated 22 December clarifying my situation.

Today I received a phone call from Jane ▮▮▮, the decision maker. She stated that she has upheld her decision to reject my claim because I was working fifty hours per week and the law allows me to work only 16 hours per week if in receipt of benefits. Whilst I have explained fully in my letter the difference between 'work' and 'employment', my status as a sole trader means that any effort I make to secure employment is actually regarded as employment. However, it is a stipulation of the Department for Work and Pensions that I had to sign a statement declaring I would make reasonable efforts to seek employment. As the gentleman at the Bath Job Centre will confirm, I exceeded my obligations to the point that he was visibly and vocally surprised at the extreme effort I had made to find work.

So, to clarify, the law states I must make an effort to find employment. However, the law also states that by making the effort to find employment I am not entitled to receive help from the state!

I spoke at length again with Judith ███████ after my conversation with Jane ████ because she is, after all, the Complaints Resolution Manager. Whilst Judith has taken every effort to listen and explain and has been both patient and respectful, she has entirely failed to fulfil her remit and resolve my complaint. She stated that she is very sorry but cannot overturn the decision and cannot help me. The law states...

Regrettably, everyone I come into contact with regarding this situation hides behind the law and fails to recognise that it is utterly absurd. Not one of you appears willing to see beyond the words on the page and listen to the truth or see reason. The welfare state was established to help those in need and it places obligations on recipients of benefits to show willingness to gain employment. In which aspect have I failed, please? Can none of you see that the law is clearly flawed when I am refused help *because* I am fulfilling my obligations? Why do you all steadfastly refuse to see reason?

I had a conversation this week with a former work colleague who has voluntarily left both of her jobs so that the state will support her as she focuses on her art. When I asked her how she could receive benefit despite her unemployment being a voluntary situation, she said, without shame, "I lied."

Furthermore, when I handed in my letter of 22 December 2012 by hand, as requested, I had to step around a small group of people who were clearly inebriated and abusive to passers by, who were also in receipt of state benefits.

I don't begrudge anyone in need of help receiving it, but please will one of you be honest enough to explain why the above examples are worthy of benefits but I am refused help and ignored by those with the power and the responsibility to help purely because I made the mistake of attempting to secure employment so that I would not need to claim aid from the state any longer than absolutely necessary?

I have learned several important lessons:

1. The state, the government, the Job Centre and the Department for Work and Pensions emphatically do not care!
2. Honesty is *never* the best policy for those in need!
3. I should have lied, I should not have looked for work and I should have stayed at home and watched daytime television rather than make an effort to be self-sufficient again.

I have no faith in any of you and I regret my honesty. I apologise for my stupidity and am ashamed that I have clearly caused you all amusement because I naïvely believed the state would help me while I was temporarily incapacitated. Will one of you please explain to me at what point those placed in positions of responsibility became consumed by bureaucracy and forgot humanity, and when it became *de rigueur* to do so?

When did it happen to *you*?

When people given power and responsibility to help those in need turn their backs, make excuses, ignore or simply refuse to assist those who they have been tasked with helping, what other course of action is open to me?

Yours sincerely,

Edward Field.

***Success rating: 2/10** – I received three letters in response. The first was from the Decision Making and Appeals Team and essentially invited me to appeal in court. The second was from Nick ████████ and included one damning sentence:*

The decision is based on the law and regulations governing the administration of JSA and we do not have the jurisdiction to change these rules.

The final response was from Jacob Rees-Mogg, MP. I duly replied.

Case Study 9d – Department for Work & Pensions

Clearly this was the end of the line. With shoulders slumped this was my parting shot. I had no hope of a satisfactory resolution, merely a desire to make clear the idiocy of a law that hinders, and is prejudiced against, those who work hardest to help themselves.

Squircle Entertainment

Not quite a square; not quite a circle...

edward@squircleentertainment.com   www.squircleentertainment.com   www.squiss.co.uk
Squircle Entertainment,
+44 (0)   Twitter: @edwardsquircle

1 February 2013

Jacob Rees-Mogg MP
House of Commons
London
SW1A 0AA

Dear Mr. Rees-Mogg

Reference: National Insurance no.
Housing/Council Tax Benefit Claim Ref:
Council Tax Reference:

Thank you for responding to my letter. As expected, both Mr. Cameron and Mr. Clegg passed the buck while Ian Duncan Smith, Lynda ▮▮▮, Paula ▮▮▮ and Judith ▮▮▮ opted to ignore it. I am grateful to you for at least taking the time to write, even if you have not resolved the issue.

I misunderstood and believed I should appeal the decision only when all other avenues had been closed. I have subsequently downloaded the form and have posted my appeal.

You mention my only other option is to reapply for JSA but please would you clarify your advice for me? You reiterate that I must be working fewer that sixteen hours per week and that I may have to 'explain the reduction in your working hours from your previous application'. The only way I can do so is to lie because I did put in many hours to find work. Are you advising me to be 'economical' with the truth, please?

You also stated 'If accepted for JSA you are required actively to look for work. This may involve searching for employment beyond your current efforts at self-employment.' As my 'current efforts' are on record as approximately fifty hours per week, what is a suitable effort to display, please? Is sixty hours per week satisfactory? If I do provide evidence of sixty hours per week, won't I then be rejected again as sixty hours is also more than sixteen hours and I remain a sole trader. Won't I be rejected as the Department for Work and Pensions appears not to understand the difference between 'work' and 'employment'?

I apologise for writing to you again, Mr. Rees-Mogg, but I am confused. It seems to me that the law, the Department for Work and Pensions and the government are all prejudiced against me for being honest. The way you and Judith ▮▮▮ have explained it, I am damned if I do and damned if I don't. If I put the effort in, I am not entitled to help; but if I don't, I will be denied assistance.

Please will you clarify this for me, as I would prefer to lie in my application for JSA knowing that I have understood the advice correctly and that I will be assisted by the Department for Work and Pensions if I do so?

So that she is kept up to date on the situation, I shall send a copy of this letter to Judith ▮▮▮.

Thank you again for your assistance and I shall look forward to hearing form you in due course.

Yours sincerely

Edward Field.

Success rating: 2/10 – I received my final letter from Jacob Rees-Mogg four days later. He said nothing new and could not change the situation but at least he did respond. In the interest of honesty and clarity, I must include a sentence from his letter:

To clarify my advice, I do not advise you to lie in any application for Job Seekers Allowance (JSA).

Ultimately, it was a disaster for me. I should have walked away as soon as I realised the law was skewed but I was led both by a desire for justice and a need to pay the rent. In such cases there is nothing for it but to sulk briefly and move on.

After ten points of contact that I can name, and five or six that I cannot, I gave up. Work came in, I began the task of clearing my overdraft and resolved to never contact the DWP or my local MP again. Painful though it was, the experience was a very valid lesson for me and I hope you are able to take something from it without having to suffer anything similar firsthand. I worried about laying so much of my soul upon the page for you to pick over, but if my misfortune helps another avoid similar anguish it is worth it.
In such circumstances I have two quotes of comfort from better men than I:

Law and order exist for the purpose of establishing justice and when they fail in this purpose they become the dangerously structured dams that block the flow of social progress - Martin Luther King, Jr.

And

If the machine of government is of such a nature that it requires you to be the agent of injustice to another, then, I say, break the law – Henry David Thoreau

Maybe I'm naïve or stupidly idealistic, but given the circumstances again, I still wouldn't lie. I stand by all that I have said about being honest. Yes, I lost a battle but I can still look at myself in the mirror.
But if you're feeling downhearted by the end of that saga, don't lose hope yet. Not every lost battle or failed conquest ends so negatively. Even if the door is slammed in your face and your complaint is dismissed completely, it is still possible to gain the upper hand and to eke out some pleasure from the experience. Frequently, *feeling* victorious is at least as good as *being* victorious.
I mentioned in Chapter 1 the power of public embarrassment and cited the success of Paddy Ashdown MP versus Medicare. But public embarrassment isn't a tool wielded solely by your MP or others in a position of authority or influence. You, too, have the power to expose the wrongs of others on a grand scale. I'm not talking about distasteful 'kiss and tell' stories that people sell to the tabloids, but if a company has wronged you and refuses to respond or take responsibility, you might not be able to beat them but you can make sure as many people as possible know exactly what they did so that, firstly, others can avoid the same treatment and, secondly, just maybe the public knowledge of the issue might sting enough for their customer relations policies to change.

As always, a word of warning: Be very, very wary of slander and libel. If it is absolutely true, there isn't much they can do about it, but make damn sure you have the evidence in your toolkit because Great & Powerful Ltd. has a heck of a lot more money than you and can afford a team of lawyers that you can only dream of. Don't go there. We're talking about complaints here, not litigation!

Be careful of how you attack, what you say and whether you open yourself up to further confrontations from other directions. If there is a flaw in your argument, if you are at all at fault and don't own up to it, they can use it against you to justify their position or nullify yours.

There is an element of 'people in glass houses...' at play here. Can you handle that? Just by writing this book, I'm fairly certain I'll receive a handful of letters complaining about my writing, the content, my shoe size, whatever. If I'm very fortunate, some of them may even be written in wax crayon. But so be it. After my run-in with British Airways, **Case Study 4**, I received a helpful attack for being an idiot (the language used was actually stronger) for leaving my car keys in my suitcase. Yes, I *was* an idiot. It was an oversight never to be repeated, but I opened myself up to the attack and have to suck it up. When complaining to, or about, a large company, there is a possibility they may respond by pointing out *your* errors and/or requesting that you shop elsewhere. Are you prepared to take that risk?

However, if you're up for the challenge and fancy a little public mischief, there is much fun to be had. It used to be that disgruntled consumers had to depend on Esther Rantzen and the *That's Life* team, *Watchdog* or a benevolent newspaper willing to run with their story. Then Sir Tim Berners-Lee came along with a great big gift to the world with the unexpected byproduct of the possibility for you to have your very own global forum from the safety of your home.

I have found the most effective public bashings are both truthful and humorous. Who wants to read a stream of vitriol during their coffee break in an already stressful office? A funny, biting, exposé that voices the angst of the silent majority and nips at the ankles of the hitherto untouchable giants, however, is a delightful accompaniment to tea and biscuits at the desk and, if it sufficiently amuses or touches a nerve, it will surely be shared and just might become viral, making you the champion of the underdog.

All you need is a valid reason to complain publically. Enter, First Great Western.

Case Study 10 – First Great Western

In November 2012, I had reason to change my rail ticket and visited Bristol Temple Meads railway station to do so as I have done on various occasions before and since, unaware that I had committed a heinous crime. The events that unfolded over the twenty minutes or so that I was at the ticket office caused a number of wide-eyed stares. There was no real apology forthcoming from the staff and not a hope of a refund or compensation for my treatment, but my website, The Squiss, has a loyal following and I needed another essay to write.

In accordance with my rules, I wrote to First Great Western's chairman, Sir Chay Blyth, attaching a copy of the article and to inform him that I would be posting it on my website in a couple of days, half expecting him to contact me, offer me an apology and request that I refrain from doing so. He didn't, so I did. You can read it, with pretty pictures, on **The Squiss***. Otherwise, here is* Happy Travels; First Great Western Hates You.

Happy Travels; First Great Western Hates You

There was a moment when I thought I would be arrested. Without realizing, I had committed a crime so serious it caused an apoplectic outburst from a highly trained and trusted member of First Great Western's personnel, the public face of the company.

From the reaction of Sue, the woman First Great Western chooses to represent the company at the Bristol Temple Meads ticket office, my offence was an horrific act of deviance the like of which I have never previously committed. The tirade she inflicted on me, *twice* stamping away into rooms unseen, the second time never to return, initially bemused me. Then it concerned me. Exactly how serious was my crime to warrant such an explosion?

My offence will shock you and may even cause you to recoil in horror.

I wrote on my ticket!

My *dead* ticket. The ticket I couldn't use. The ticket I needed to exchange, with a small fee, for another ticket.

I didn't scrawl obscene symbols or insignia over it; I didn't write offensive statements; I didn't even scribble expletives across the ticket. What I wrote was:

Change to 10:30
↓
12:15

For those failing to understand my satanic code, it's the departure and arrival time of the train I needed to catch in order to reach my job in London, my initial call time having been brought forward an hour. It was my personal reminder to buy the correct ticket this time.

Previously when I've exchanged tickets, it has been a simple, pleasant transaction incurring a £10 charge and approximately two minutes of my time. How naïve of me to expect the same.

To be fair, Sue's first words were a very pleasant, "Next please."

I explained the situation, handed over my ticket and credit card and…

Sue snatched it away and screeched "You've defaced it!"

She kept repeating the line in the same way one might exclaim "You've decapitated my hamster!"

Bewilderment set in. I explained it was a dead ticket, *my* dead ticket that I had paid for and therefore owned. *My* unusable ticket to do with as I please.

Apparently that did not compute in Sue's world and clearly didn't fit in with the laws of First Great Western. She glared, snapped and all but screamed at me in case I was in any doubt as to how wicked my actions had been. Flippantly, I suggested if my crime was that severe she should summon the transport police to deal with me.

Without warning or reduction of hysteria, Sue stormed off for the first time without any explanation or indication of where she was going or when she might return.

My surprise subsided and I looked around to see if there were cameras and I was the subject of a new version of *Trigger Happy TV*. Surely it had to be a joke. Nobody could react with such rancour, such unreasonable, unprompted aggression simply because I wrote two words, four numbers and an arrow on a ticket. Sue's reaction was so ridiculous, so utterly absurd, it had to be a comedy sketch. Didn't it?

The viciousness of her return dispelled those fanciful thoughts. She glowered at me and again repeated her mantra.

"You've defaced it! You'll have to buy another ticket."

No amount of explanation could encourage her to be reasonable and so I gave up trying and held out my credit card again with one more request.

"May I have it back please?"

Sue's reaction couldn't have been more venomous if I'd declared a desire to immolate her firstborn. She snatched the offending ticket far out of reach and stepped back.

"NO! You can't have it. You've defaced it!"

"It's mine. I paid for it. I need it for my accounts. Are you going to explain to the Inland Revenue why I don't have my receipts?"

"You can't have it!"

A hint of red mist passed before me.

"The ticket's mine. If you refuse to give it back, it's theft. I want to see your…"

My last word was lost in the stamping of feet as Sue thundered into the great void beyond the door, never to be seen again. Once again I was left alone in the ticket office with no idea of what the next development would be. The minutes past, my next appointment looked to be a lost cause and the red mist thickened around me.

Behind another counter sat a colleague of Sue's, so I attempted to explain and ask if she knew where my tormentor had gone. With an incredulous stare, as if I were deranged, she barked, "To get a manager."

So I waited.

And waited.

Until, finally, Tom, the duty Station Manager, arrived with feeble excuses for Sue's verbal attack and confirmation that I had indeed committed a crime. At my request, he produced a photocopy of National Rail's *Conditions of Carriage*. On page 13, section D, item 23 it does indeed state *If a ticket has been damaged or has been tampered with or altered in any way, it is not valid for travel.*

However, my ticket was not damaged. Not even the corners were dented. It had not been tampered with. The Oxford English Dictionary states *tamper: meddle with or make unauthorized changes in.* It had not been altered. I had not attempted to forge or amend it to fool First Great Western staff and I did not intend to use it for travel! I had simply written a note on it for myself.

More to the point, how would I know about page 13, section D, item 23 of the *Conditions of Carriage*? Has any passenger *ever* been given it and instructed to read it prior to purchasing tickets? I certainly haven't. Tom's response was a shrug and a statement that was supposed to resolve everything.

"It's there if you look for it on the website."

In 1979, Douglas Adams published *The Hitchhiker's Guide to the Galaxy*, from which this scenario appears to have been lifted. On discovering his home is about to be bulldozed to make way for a bypass, Arthur Dent is informed the plans were available to him to read and dispute if only he'd searched in the bottom of a locked filing cabinet in a dark cellar. Adams continues with the destruction of the Earth by the Vogons to make way for a hyperspace express route. And, yes, the plans had been made available to read for fifty years. On Alpha Centuri.

The thing is, in Douglas Adams' case, it was funny.

But it's okay because Tom gave me an A4 pamphlet entitled *Tell Us Your Views* so that I may complain. Inside is a box measuring approximately 8cm x 15cm for customers to lodge their complaints and post to First Great Western's customer services department to be ignored. Well, that's all right then.

So as long as we all behave ourselves and accept that First Great Western is, based on the public face of its staff, aggressive, reactionary, extreme, hysterical, without a sense of logic and utterly unreasonable, we should be fine. I feel perfectly safe on trains that are driven by staff members who meet their exacting standards.

But what worries me now is that I scribbled a note to myself on one of their brochures. And what happens if on the train tomorrow I hold my cardboard cup inappropriately or allow a foot to stray into the aisle? Are there more laws of which I am unaware that may lead to a public dismemberment at the hands of another First Great Western gauleiter?

Travel safely. First Great Western hates you.

Another diatribe from The Squiss.
Like the Facebook page: http://on.fb.me/RpitOG

Success rating: **10/10** – *This wasn't about compensation and I didn't receive any. This was about sharing an experience, exposing the truth and having fun with it. I received plenty of emails from readers who enjoyed the article and some from people who had endured similar experiences. Whilst it didn't go viral, it was one of my most successful articles on the website at the time and still enjoys a trickle of hits from people Googling 'I hate First Great Western.' It transpires there are quite a few* *of them out there.*

Sometimes it is worth suffering a brief indignity to enjoy the pleasure gained from a striking comeback. But whether you want justice, compensation or just an opportunity to let rip across the page, you need a valid reason and if you're struggling to find one, I have a few ideas for you.

Chapter 6: Reasons to Rage

There are some for whom everything in life is peachy. There are those for whom nothing goes awry, nothing is mis-sold, all orders arrive as expected and a charmed life is spent basking in a glow of Turkish Delight-scented rose. If that sums up your life, I'm not quite sure why you are reading a book about complaining effectively unless it is to see how the unfortunate many wander through life, in which case enjoy your smugness, move on and leave the rest of us to clamour for your good fortune. But if you haven't complained, have always wanted to complain but just couldn't find the reason to complain, well that's another matter.

In Chapter 8, *Complaining for Fun*, I'll introduce you to the most enjoyable aspects of letter writing and complaining and to some of the people who would inspire me to complain for the sheer joy of it if I had the time. For now, let's look at the rosy glow of ignorant contentment surrounding you - and dispel it. It isn't real. There are reasons to rage all around you if only you care to see them.

I'm not going to get all political and moralistic on you and suggest you lobby Parliament about the wars and injustices in the Middle East, the 842 million hungry people (according to the World Food Programme) in the world or the political prisoners in the east and west. Yes, we should all involve ourselves in taking responsibility for all the injustices in the world that *really* matter, but Noam Chomsky says it better and Amnesty International, Greenpeace and Sea Shepherd *do* it a lot better than I can.

I'm here to deal with the issues around you that, while not destroying your world, certainly disrupt the flow of it. If you haven't found reason, you're not looking hard enough! Too often complaining is about the expectation of reward when it should be about letting off steam lest your head explode with the build up of boiling blood. Why let anything ruin your day? If something has upset you that could and should have been avoided, write a letter about it. Let somebody else worry about it.

Let's start with an old friend for **Case Study 11**. In my best Voice of God announcement, please welcome to the stage to collect the award for Greatest Cause of Constant Frustration, Cineworld!

Oh, man, they wind me up! Before I launch into my explanatory tirade, let me qualify it with some complimentary notes first. My Cineworld cinema of choice is Hengrove Park in Bristol. It is convenient, it is the closest cinema to me, they show all of the big, studio movies and a few of the smaller, independent films and they offer the Unlimited card, which gives the subscribers frequent advance screenings. It is mostly clean, their aversion to providing soap aside, and I've learnt that, such is the local demographic, if I see the blockbusters early in the week or before 5pm and save Fridays and the weekends for the foreign and independent films I can usually enjoy an auditorium less than half full and very occasionally have it to myself. More than that, the staff members are generally excellent. Many of them recognise me due to my 100+ visits per year, they are good at what they do, friendly and, if it isn't too busy, frequently stop to chat about films and compare notes.

I *like* Cineworld.

But...

Case Study 11 – Cineworld Cinemas

There was nothing to be gained from this letter to the chairman. Mostly I've just bitten my tongue or tweeted about the latest own goal from the Cineworld head office or screening box in the back end of nowhere, but by July 2014 I had tucked away too many niggling issues and the arrival of allocated seating was the last straw. I had no expectation of a change in policy or even an understanding reply. I just needed to yell and somebody needed to hear it.

Squircle Entertainment
Not quite a square; not quite a circle...

edward@squircleentertainment.com   www.squircleentertainment.com   www.squiss.co.uk
Squircle Entertainment,
+44 (0) ███████   Twitter: @edwardsquircle

1 July 2014

Mr. Anthony Herbert Bloom, Chairman
Cineworld Group plc
███████

Dear Mr. Bloom

In January of last year I wrote to you regarding issues with my wife's and my Cineworld Unlimited cards. It was an ongoing saga that took a good eighteen months to resolve. Until it resurfaced recently. I felt reluctant to contact you again about recent problems but you preside over Cineworld Group plc and who else is going to take the matters seriously if the chairman doesn't?

The Unlimited cards problem might have finally been resolved (again) with the cancelling of our accounts and the creation of new accounts. But that's small fry.

Cineworld was our preferred choice of cinema in Bristol but is rapidly becoming the institution that killed the joy of film viewing and only you can reverse the trend.

I understand why you dispensed with the projectionists: money. But it was a terrible decision. Forget the employment issue, there is now no one to take responsibility and rectify problems immediately. When I was a projectionist at a 16mm cinema club, my pre-show checks included running not just the titles but the first few minutes of the film to ensure the correct aspect ratio was selected, that the audio levels were suitable and that the image was crisp. Now, at Cineworld, when the image is soft, when the wrong lens is selected or when our ears hurt from the audio levels, we have to wait until the manager is found, phone calls are made to the screening location and somebody, somewhere decides whether to make changes many, many miles away from the screening we have attended. On one recent occasion, the assistant manager came into the auditorium to hear for himself and we had to literally shout at each other in order to be heard. When he phoned the central office, the response was apparently "The levels look alright here."

A real, human projectionist would simply step out of his or her booth, stand in the auditorium and experience what we, the paying viewers, are contending with.

But I'm not naïve; I know you have dispensed with projectionists for good. There is no hope there but perhaps there is still time for the other issues...

One of the bonuses of being an Unlimited card holder (and I have been almost since their inception) is the regular exclusive screenings. Would you like to hear about our experiences in Bristol (and presumably elsewhere)?

The Secret Life of Walter Mitty: With the screening due to start, the lights remained on and the screen remained black. For almost an hour and without explanation or apology. Then, when it finally started, the quality was so unbelievably unwatchable (it appeared to have been bleached and mashed through a cheese grater), that approximately 95% of the attendees walked out en masse. The hard core ten or so of us remained, the film faltered, the lights came up, staff wandered aimlessly around the auditorium and eventually, almost 90 minutes late, The Secret Life of Walter Mitty was reborn.

The Raid 2 – Berandal: The screening proceeded perfectly and on time, but for the omission of subtitles, and concluded minutes later with the complete crash of the film. On a lighter note, it did prompt the following gem from one of the knuckle draggers who had made it past security: "Oh, it's froze. 'E ain't talking Chinese no more..."

Blue Ruin: This one was almost as good. There was no print, no screening, no apology, no making amends.

Beyond that, frequently Bristol is omitted from the Unlimited screenings list. Why are we not worthy of *all* the films the other Cineworld cinemas screen?

There is another unfortunate bi-product of the Unlimited screenings. As it stands, you allow just one booking on the Unlimited card at a time. I average ten films per month and often see more than one film per day. I realise I am a long way from the numbers achieved by Mark Kermode, with whom I shall also raise this issue in the hope he has more influence that I, but it is sufficient to have a broad experience of Cineworld and other cinemas. I live in a village several miles out of Bristol and so rely on the internet booking system. If I wish to book two films I must either make a special trip in to book my tickets and then return to see the films or take a chance on queues and availability when I arrive. If, in the case of the Unlimited screenings, I book my tickets immediately so as not to miss out, I am then faced with the prospect of up to a month of being unable to book another ticket online.

Which brings us to the latest debacle: allocated seating.

I come from a time where the early bird catches the worm. I work in an industry where if I am less than five minutes early, I am late. Previously, for those who made the effort to arrive early, the best seats could be secured while those who live a life of tardiness had to make do with craning their necks in the front row. I used to be able to choose my seats so that I didn't have to struggle to see around the giant in front or try to block out the conversations and misbehavior of the selfish. Now, regardless of how early I arrive, I must suffer whatever nuisance is seated beside or in front of me, even if the cinema is only 25% full. I must deal with the noise and disturbance of those who cannot be bothered to arrive on time but who need to traipse past or sit in front of me, taking their time to settle and blocking my view. There is now no escape and no incentive to arrive early.

Furthermore, with the inability to book multiple tickets on my Unlimited card, I am prevented from booking tickets far enough in advance to avoid the inconsiderate.

With reference to my previous letter, I cannot be bothered to raise the issue of a constant lack of soap in the toilets. I have now accepted that Cineworld Bristol assumes I am unhygienic.

I think part of the issue may be that I am not a texting, chattering, popcorn-munching, easily pleased moviegoer; I have the misfortune of being a lover of film and of the pure cinema experience. I'm one of those sad creatures who reads about and researches the films, who watches (and enjoys) the credits and the incidental music, who takes pride in the eclectic taste displayed on my DVD shelf; you know, the kind of film enthusiast you'd find at the BFI Southbank *and* at the local multiplex. I am equally at ease watching big budget blockbusters and quirky independent films regardless of language, director, star or studio. I embrace the quality, irrespective of genre, that begins on the screenwriter's page and concludes in the cinema's auditorium. I love the experience of film and cinema but Cineworld is in grave danger of killing it.

Alas, I don't expect you to care or make any changes. I am but one person with a monthly direct debit to enjoy films amongst the noisy hoards who go out to 'see a movie'. However, I do look forward to your response.

Yours sincerely

Edward Field.

Success rating: 6/10 – I did actually receive an email in response from Mr. Bloom and, though he understandably defended Cineworld's position regarding projectionists, he informed me that the restrictions on pre-booking would be changed. Since writing the letter, Unlimited black card holders may now book three films in advance in addition to any Unlimited special screenings, although I am not claiming any credit for the change in policy. Top marks to Cineworld for that.

Mostly, though, the success rating is due to my own wellbeing. I said it, I wrote it and it is no longer in the back of my mind nibbling at my brain.

If you are not a fan of the new allocated seat system either, there's a complaint you can make. If enough people shout loudly enough, policies can be changed. On the subject of cinemas, there is a whole raft of complaints waiting for your attention:

The lack of ushers or staff inside the auditorium to maintain standards and prevent inconsiderate behaviour (or, in The Watershed's case, the pointlessness of having them in there when they don't intervene); failure to clamp down on talking/phoning/texting during films; switching the lights on or switching the film off before the credits have finished; confectionary served in noisy bags – why, oh why, if they need to generate profits by selling confectionery, can they not at least serve it in soft, silent cloth bags that can then be returned and reused in exchange for the repayment of a deposit?

Stepping away from cinemas, if you are looking for a challenge to sink your teeth into feel free to run with some of these:

- Inconsiderate behaviour in the designated Quiet Coach on trains. The journalist, Bidisha, had a good attempt at resolving it in the Huffington Post but nothing has improved so far.
- Passengers taking vast suitcases and multiple bags as carry-on luggage on aeroplanes, despite the restrictions, and airlines doing nothing about it.
- Refuse collectors refusing to pick up rubbish in the wrong bags, refusing to pick up too many bags, not picking up the rubbish they spill...
- The FA's lack of ability to produce a national team and coach that threatens to gather trophies in our lifetime. There's an entire chapter of solutions just waiting to be written.
- The lack of promotion of our women's and under 21s teams. Why not take the old cinema approach and have 'b-matches' before the main event? Often the matches would be better than the headline game and the 'b-teams' would enjoy bigger crowds than they currently do.
- The speed limit on our motorways. Whichever way you lean, there's a complaint in there.
- Cyclists riding on pavements. Roads are for wheels; pavements are for feet. Simple!
- HS2. With an estimated cost of £46.2 BILLION (!!!) that looks likely to increase (again), the loss of more countryside and the threat to property values versus the saving of 30 minutes travel time for those

comparatively few people who will make the journey anyway, why can we find the money for this but *not* to tackle homelessness, fund the hospitals, equip the schools, subsidise public transport, fund the renewable energy projects that could fuel us for eons, or, heck, have a bloody great party that EVERYONE could benefit from?

• Our energy crises. Coal versus nuclear energy versus hydropower versus solar power versus wind power versus fracking versus dynamos versus... There must be *something* in there that gets your goat.

• Parliament and the political system. Likewise, if you cannot find something within this quagmire worth complaining about, you're probably not breathing.

• The lack of 'fuel only' queues at petrol stations with mini supermarkets attached.

• Enforcement of the '10 items or less' tills.

• The misuse of 'less' when 'fewer' should be used.

• Spelling mistakes, grammatical errors, mixed upper and lower case letters, the omission of apostrophes on shop/street signs. Again, there are enough 'misuse of English' complaints to be made to fill a book all on its own, just ask Lynne Truss: devastated, see-through, decimated, literally, I could care less... Arrrggghhh!

• Litter in our towns and on our waterways.

• Public exposure of beer bellies on our streets in the summer.

• Illegal obstruction of cycle lanes.

• Local councils' obsessions with road signs that state the obvious and what we should have learned for our driving test: No fly tipping, do not stop in the box junction etc.

• Hotels that switch on the air conditioning instead of switching off the heating.

• Windows that are bolted closed i.e. the prohibition of natural, free, eco-friendly air conditioning.

• Supermarkets that stack the top shelves too high to reach.

• Traffic wardens. Period.

• Paid parking in hospitals. As if watching a loved one in pain isn't bad enough.

• Hospitals that provide personal Patientline TVs, phones and internet connection at the bedside – for extortionate fees.

• Pressure (justly applied!) to recycle domestically while industry, conferences and exhibitions are a disaster area. When was the last time *you* wandered around an exhibition centre 30 minutes after it closed and observed the piles of discarded stands, mountains of wood and miles of carpet destined for landfill?

• Barbecuing/partying/playing music in public. There must be at least two sides to this hot potato.

- The excessive display of national flags on houses, shops, buildings and cars whenever there is an international sporting tournament. Or when there is a 'y' in the day.
- Apologies made for or restrictions on flying the national flag because it has been hijacked by an odious, extremist, jingoistic political group.
- Food wastage. How many hungry, homeless people do you know that care if the carrot is wonky, the potato is ugly or the pie is one day (or a week!) past its absurd 'use by' date? And what of the piles of leftover food in restaurants? Add to that people who pile up their plates at 'all you can eat' buffets and leave half of it rather than taking small amounts and returning often.
- For that matter, restaurants that serve only one size of meal thereby increasing food wastage.
- Excessive use of Christmas lights in residential areas.
- Christmas arriving in September, Easter arriving in January and 'Back to School' promotions before the children have even broken up.
- Playgrounds and parks where adults are not allowed to join in the fun.
- Cotton wool for humans: Prevention of tree climbing, river swimming, conker playing, race running etc. in case someone falls, trips, slips, bounces or loses.
- Political correctness that defies logic or reason.
- Councils cutting hedgerows either in the spring, thereby killing all the buds and new growth, or in the early autumn and wiping out all the berries thereby preventing my, sorry, *your* production of blackberry jam, sloe gin and elderberry wine and destroying the principal food source of our birds and other wildlife.
- City folk messing with the countryside. I say reintroduce elk, wolves, lynx and brown bears!

Still don't know what to complain about?

There is a very good chance that some of you will disagree with my thoughts and opinions on some of these suggestions and have opinions of your own. That's perfectly fine with me, just don't complain to me because I can't do anything about it. Write to someone who can!

Whatever you choose to complain about, whether it has far-reaching consequences or not, it helps to feel passionately about it. The vehemence of your stance will come across in your writing and, if you're going to complain about something, you might as well enjoy it.

And so it was with Kybotech.

Case Study 12 – Kybotech

This was another letter I wrote for someone else. As with the Cineworld letter, Case Study 11, Matt had no expectation of a response and wanted nothing as compensation, but was mightily cheesed off by the ineptitude of Kybotech's staff and the company's attitude to customer service. With both him and his wife having had their days messed about, Matt wanted somebody to understand the frustration caused through what should have been a straightforward transaction.

Bristol

12 July 2008

Charles Walton, Managing Director
Kybotech Ltd.

Dear Mr. Walton

Please would you be kind enough to express my sincerest gratitude to Graham in your Customer Care department. Today the slide arrived for my two young daughters and they will be delighted with it. Graham has proved to be the solitary bright light in the darkest oubliette that is Kybotech.

My relationship with Kybotech has lasted for too many arduous weeks to count during which my patience has been stretched to the limits. If I ran my company, ███████████████ Ltd. in the way that Kybotech appears to operate I am certain that I would be seeking a new vocation within a very short period.

My original order was very simple: a climbing frame complete with swing and slide. My order was accepted, the delivery date was arranged, I paid the required fee and regarded the contract in place. At no point have I reneged on my part of our business deal.

When the delivery date arrived, I made provision to be working from home in order to accept it. However I waited in vain. When I telephoned Kybotech to enquire as to why the play equipment I had paid for had not been delivered, I found myself fourteenth in the queue and waited in line, at *my* expense in terms of time and my telephone bill, until I reached sixth position and was then cut off. I repeated the call *four times* until I was finally successful in reaching a person with whom I could talk. Unfortunately, the member of staff I spoke to was abrupt and offensive and refused to accept any responsibility whatsoever for Kybotech's error.

Eventually he informed me that the slide was out of stock and would remain so for another week. Three weeks later I made a further *six* attempts to contact Kybotech, each time waiting in a queue of thirteen people for at least thirty minutes and each time being cut off.

When I did finally reach a human rather than a recording, I was assured that the equipment would be delivered.

It was. But not as ordered or promised.

Alas, somebody at Kybotech mistook my order for a *blue slide measuring approximately eight feet* for a box of rungs for a climbing wall. Needless to say, my two-year-old may struggle with climbing a wall at this stage and so I was forced to make further calls and arrange collection and delivery of a slide, as per my original order. Notes were made that it was an urgent delivery and that extra care should be taken.

On the agreed delivery date, my wife took time off work to wait. She waited all day. Why? Because the delivery personnel noticed that the slide was faulty and returned to the depot but didn't see any reason to call my wife to inform her of the situation!

Deciding that your Customer Care department was both ineffectual and a statement of irony, I contacted Companies House to obtain a new telephone number via which I could have a reasonable conversation with an intelligent human who might actually display some consideration for the very customers that keep Kybotech in business. Fortunately, I reached Graham. He apologised for the previous problems with your telephone system and stated that the whole system had been affected by a power cut. I accepted his explanation but question the state of your technology if ten of my calls can be cut off due to power failures.

Graham has fulfilled all of his promises and the slide has just arrived as originally ordered. I am extremely grateful to Graham and he must be commended for his professionalism and attitude. However, I am left with certain questions:

Why, when I honoured my side of our contract, has Kybotech singularly failed to keep its side, failed to accept any responsibility and steadfastly refused to offer any compensation?

Why do you have insufficient staff to answer the telephones so that customers who obviously need assistance are further infuriated by the inordinate wait, expense incurred and the complete failure, in most instances, to actually connect the call to your customer care department?

Why has Kybotech failed to take ownership of this dire state of affairs, failed to make a formal and honest apology and refused to make amends in any way?

What possible reason is there for me to make further purchases from Kybotech, recommend your company and products to others or refrain from highlighting the travesty that is Kybotech?

I look forward to your thoughts and response.

Yours sincerely

Matt █
Managing Director
████████████████ Ltd.

Success rating: 7/10 – As expected, there was no gift and little more than a standard letter in response claiming that Matt's thoughts and suggestions had been duly considered. It mattered not. All that counted was that Matt could move on and I had the pleasure of unloading his angst onto a couple of sheets of paper and sending it elsewhere.

So there we are. No excuses. There *is* a reason for you to complain. The first letter is the hardest but fire that off and before long you'll be a seasoned expert looking for the next reason to rage. All it takes to start your campaign is some courage and a toolkit.

Chapter 7: The Complainer's Toolkit

We have established that you have been wronged, that you have good reason to complain and now you've psyched yourself up and are ready to rage.

STOP!

Time for a checklist. We've been through some of this already, so I'll lay it out with a bullet-pointed list as an easy reference for you. I have endeavoured to provide the full web and page links for you to type in, otherwise just enter the search terms and use my text as a reference for your intended destination. Feel free to photocopy and enlarge the forms, and copy the template. Easy peasy. Let's go.

Dos and Don'ts

- **Do** ensure you have a valid reason to complain.
- **Do** be a **SAD FART**: **S**atisfactory quality, **A**s **D**escribed, **F**it for purpose **A**nd last a **R**easonable length of **T**ime. See Martin Lewis, the Money Saving Expert, for more details.
- **Do** complain as soon as possible. Don't let it fester and cease to be relevant.
- **Do** have all the relevant information to hand.
- **Do** give yourself a slap across the **CHoPPS**: **C**larity, **Ho**nesty, **P**reparation, **P**resentation, **S**olution.
- **Don't** use obscenities or expletives in any method of complaint unless quoting directly – and then only with great care.
- **Don't** phone while you're angry.
- **Do** write your letter when you're angry, but...
- **Don't** post it! Wait, reread it, edit and post 24 hours later.
- **Do** make notes of all names, phone numbers and promises etc.
- **Do** follow up your email, letter or phone call.
- **Do** keep copies of all your correspondence for future reference.
- **Do** act within the law.
- **Don't** slander or libel anyone.
- **Do** tell the truth. Fraud will *not* improve your day!
- **Don't** take it out on the call centre staff.
- **Do** go directly to the organ grinder if your complaint is serious.
- **Do** make use of all the resources open to you, including you local MP – Make him/her work for his/her salary!
- **Do** have a plan and resolution in mind.
- **Don't** give up if they ignore you at first.
- **Don't** let it ruin your day.
- **Do** enjoy your victories.
- **Do** rage, but do so calmly, rationally, meaningfully and *never* in wax crayon.

Top Ten Scoundrels (in my experience)

1. **Utility Warehouse** – I have neither the space nor the inclination to repeat the saga. Horrible, horrible, horrible!
   Quality Control (effectiveness of customer service): **0/10** Never, ever again!

2. **Department for Work & Pensions** – Why change a deeply flawed law when you can hide behind it? I sincerely hope I never have to deal with the DWP again and pity anyone who must.
   Quality Control: **0/10** Refused to see reason and failed me completely.

3. **First Great Western** – Too much call for too many letters, too little customer care on display, no effort to enforce the rules of the Quiet Carriage, no satisfactory resolutions (beyond the occasional free ticket for a repeat performance) and no evidence of improvement or of intent to improve standards and performance.
   Quality Control: **5/10** The trains are clean, mostly on time and, alas, a necessity. Refunds are sometimes given.

4. **Kybotech** – Ineptitude personified.
   Quality Control: **3/10** The product, when it finally arrived, was fine but why go through that pain a second time?

5. **Heathrow Airport** – General attitude of 'it's nothing to do with us.'
   Quality Control: **2/10** Fine airport, poor attitude.

6. **Cineworld cinemas** – Emails using the online form and letters to customer services are generally ignored, issues take months and months of repeated letters and phone calls to resolve, special screenings are frequently a disaster, the audio is often wayward and then there's the introduction of allocated seating.
   Quality Control: **6/10** Good cinema with painful flaws and no real alternative locally. For the most part, dealing with the Cineworld monster beyond the Bristol cinema is challenging.

7. **Somerfield** – Complete failure to respond to correspondence, failure to accept responsibility and no attempt to make amends.
   Quality Control: **0/10** Rare need for complaints, which is just as well, but the score represents the response received.

8. **Westminster Parking Services** – No space for the letter in this edition but my experience was of an opportunistic traffic warden who lied and refused to see reason as we unloaded flight cases from a van directly outside Claridges into their ballroom.
   Quality Control: **5/10** I won because all the evidence supported my appeal and they saw reason, but it was a pointless waste of my time and a fruitless, money-grabbing exercise from them.

9. **B&NES (Bath & North East Somerset) refuse collection** – If there are too many bags they won't take them. If the sacks are not black they won't take them. If the sacks split they won't pick up the spilled rubbish. If there is too much cardboard for recycling they won't take it. If they see you

emerging from the house with rubbish/recycling, they will ignore you and drive on. If...

Quality Control: **4/10** Mostly it runs smoothly, but it's hard work dealing with such arrogance first thing on a Wednesday morning and personal responses are hard to come by from them.

10. **Sevylor** – I love my kayaks. At our level they are a fab, easy and enjoyable – unless somebody splits the valve. Getting Sevylor to respond to emails, return phone calls or provide information on how and where to buy a replacement floor bladder is about as much fun and equally as successful as milking a gnat. I'm sure it is possible, but I can think of better ways to spend my life.

    Quality Control: **0/10** The only response I received passed the buck to a distributor further down the food chain. My request that, if they wouldn't sell to me directly, they actually supply the bladder to the middleman was met with silence. It doesn't inspire me to spend money with them when I'm ready to upgrade our kayaks.

    Honourable Mention: British Telecom: Things go wrong. I accept that. I cannot, however, tolerate spending hours of my time running up my mobile phone bill by phoning their many premium rate telephone numbers, all of which lead to the same call centre in India, just because they steadfastly refuse to allow me to speak to a human being in the department dealing with my failed service in the same country that the issue is occurring!

    At time of publication, I am dealing with an ongoing 'challenge'. After brief research, the Internet appears to be littered with posts from BT customers railing against the same frustrating lack of care and service. By the second edition of *Permission to Rage*, I should have a more detailed account and a conclusion to present to you.

See Chapter 9, *Permission to Praise*, for my Top Ten Heroes (in my experience).

Useful Resources - Research

This is far from an exhaustive list but it is a starting point for your research.

Google – www.google.com
I know it's obvious, but use it. Other search engines are available, of course, but it is BIG, expansive, simple to remember AND has pretty pictures!

Money Saving Expert – www.moneysavingexpert.com
Martin Lewis, BBC's resident advice guru. The first port of call for consumer advice, discounts, deals and vouchers. An invaluable resource.

Statutory Rights - **Money Saving Expert** –
http://blog.moneysavingexpert.com/2011/07/04/this-does-not-affect-your-statutory-rights-what-it-really-means/
More from Martin Lewis. Being a SAD FART and knowing your statutory rights.

CEO Email - http://www.ceoemail.com/
This is a fairly recent discovery for me. In case there's any confusion over its purpose, it offers a list of emails for the CEOs of companies around the world. If all else fails, play with the company's email formula. Most have them e.g. forename.surname.co.uk

Companies House - http://www.companieshouse.gov.uk/index.shtml
The link above will take you to the home page. However, the following, http://www.companieshouse.gov.uk/toolsToHelp/findCompanyInfo.shtml will take you to the WebCheck page that will allow you to search company records and obtain the info you need for £1 per search.

Find your MP - http://findyourmp.parliament.uk/
The Parliament website has an awful lot of info whether you need something specific or are just trawling for personal education. To find or confirm your local MP, click the link, enter your postcode/town/partial name of your MP etc. and voilà!
The postal address for any MP is:

House of Commons
London
SW1A 0AA

Find your MSP - http://www.scottish.parliament.uk/msps.aspx
The Scottish version.

Find your Welsh AM - http://www.assemblywales.org/memhome.htm
How to find your Assembly Member.

Find your Northern Irish AM - http://www.niassembly.gov.uk/Your-MLAs/
How to find your Assembly Member.

Find your Northern Irish MP - http://www.nidirect.gov.uk/find-your-local-mp-member-of-parliament
How to find your MP.

Find your MEP - http://www.europarl.org.uk/en/your_meps.html
This one is a little more cumbersome but if you know which region you live in, the various options are revealed and you can scan through the list of MEPs until you

find yours.

Find your local councillor -
http://local.direct.gov.uk/LDGRedirect/index.jsp?LGSL=358&
Again, this is pretty easy. Enter your town or postcode and you'll be whisked off to your local council's website where you should be able to locate your councillors and the various departments dealing with all local issues.

Local councils –
https://www.gov.uk/understand-how-your-council-works/types-of-council
The www.gov.uk website is also another fantastic resource. The homepage offers links to various departments, but the main link above takes you straight to the local councils page. It even has a 'complain about your council' tab that, when you enter your postcode, also reveals the council to which you should direct your ire.

CAB: Citizens Advice Bureau - http://www.citizensadvice.org.uk/
The website for all things CAB. There's a box on the home page to enter your postcode for details of your local CAB. I have to admit I have not used the CAB for many years but have heard that governmental spending cuts have made it very difficult to book an appointment and demand is very high. Apparently, at some CABs in London, people queue up for several hours before the doors open in the hope of gaining a slot. Good luck!

CAS - Citizens Advice Scotland - http://www.cas.org.uk/
Scotland's own version of the CAB.

Citizens Information - http://www.citizensinformation.ie/en/
And for Ireland.

Ombudsman Directory Worldwide – http://www.locateombudsman.com
When you need to report a company or escalate your complaint, the word 'ombudsman' is often bandied about. Here's how you find the relevant one for your case.

Which - http://www.which.co.uk/
Many issues can be avoided by researching your purchase first and reading the reviews. There are thousands of websites out there, but this is a good start. If looking elsewhere, and I'd advise reading multiple reviews on numerous sites first, beware of fake reviews. Many people say they haven't got time to waste on reading reviews. That's certainly their prerogative, but why on earth would you willingly give your hard-earned cash to a stranger without first checking that it is a good investment?

Useful Resources - Tools

Oxford English Dictionary & Thesaurus – http://www.oed.com/
My weapon of choice. If only I could rid my computer of its inbuilt system and replace it with this.

OED Grammar - http://www.oxforddictionaries.com/words/grammar
While you're on the OED website, a quick click brings you to this, the essentials of grammar. There are plenty of good books out there, but this is a fab resource, it's on my 'favourites' tab on the toolbar and is a quick, simple resource.

Say No to 0870 - http://www.saynoto0870.com
Online resource to save you money by providing local rate alternatives to the money-grabbing premium phone numbers many companies advertise.

Please Press 1 - http://www.pleasepress1.com/uk/
Enter the company phone number you are dialing to find all the menu options so that you don't need to listen to each one in their entirety.

BBC Skillwise - http://www.bbc.co.uk/skillswise/topic-group/writing
Good old Auntie has all manner of resources on her website, including these short videos and info packs on letter writing, completing forms, grammar etc. It's a good starting point if you're uncertain.

Using English: formal letter writing -
http://www.usingenglish.com/resources/letter-writing.php
Another good reference point for laying out your letter. However, as I mentioned in Chapter 3, *Preparing for Battle*, there are many and various 'accepted' rules for writing a letter and the rules change frequently. The more sites you look at, the more confused you'll become. Compare the date's position on the above website to this one, http://www.dailywritingtips.com/how-to-format-a-uk-business-letter/ I would say don't get too hung up on it. If it looks presentable, and is not riddled with typos and grammatical errors, the content will matter most. Besides, you are complaining about *their* service, you are not sending your work to be graded by your English teacher!

Templates

1. **Complaint Process Log**
2. **Telephone Complaint Log**
3. **Standard Letter**

Complaint Process Log

Subject of Your Complaint:

Date of Incident:

Firstly, slap yourself around the **CHoPPS:**

Clarity, **Ho**nesty, **P**reparation, **P**resentation, **S**olution

Clarity:
(What happened?)

Honesty:
(Whose fault is it? Details of why you are NOT at fault e.g. instructions followed etc.)

Preparation:
(What/when/where/why/who?)

Contact name:

Contact address/email/phone number:

What you want to say:
(Buzzwords/phrases, significant information etc.)

Presentation:
(Form/s your complaint will take, pros & cons of each, notes for each paragraph,
who can proofread/check your argument & letter before you phone/post/email etc.)

1

Solution:
(What do you want them to do about this? When?)

Date of first complaint: **Format/s of first complaint:**

Response:
(Reasons/excuses made, person referred to, promises made, plan of action promised etc.)

Follow up:
(Was it resolved, do you need to escalate, who/how/where do you go from here etc.)

Date of second complaint: **Format/s of second complaint:**

Response:
(Reasons/excuses made, person referred to, promises made, plan of action promised etc.)

Follow up:
(Was it resolved, do you need to escalate, who/how/where do you go from here etc.)

2

Telephone Complaint Log

Company name: **Telephone number:**

Contact name: **Alternative number:**

Additional contact:

Date of first contact: **Time of first contact:**

Duration of call:

Notes:
(Reasons/excuses made, person referred to, promises made, plan of action promised etc.)

Follow up:
(When should they call, when should I call back, new contact name/number etc.)

Date of second contact: **Time of second contact:**

Duration of call:

Notes:
(Reasons/excuses made, person referred to, promises made, plan of action promised etc.)

Follow up:
(When should they call, when should I call back, new contact name/number etc.)

Your name
1st line of address
2nd line of address
Town/city
County
Postcode

Date

Recipient's name & job title
Company name
1st line of address
2nd line of address
Town/city
County
Postcode

Recipient's email address
NB: This is my preference, not a rule, as it keeps all the information in one place. I include this only if emailing a copy of the letter.

Dear Name OR Dear Sir or Madam OR To Whom It May Concern
NB: It is ALWAYS preferable to have a name and a person in mind if you wish to be taken seriously!

Reference number or relevant heading

Introduction paragraph: Who you are and why you are complaining. One paragraph will usually suffice.

Explanation paragraphs: What went wrong, why it happened, what upset you and the chronology of the incident or incidents. This is the bulk of the letter and so may run into many paragraphs.

Reasoning paragraph: Why this should not have happened and what you would have expected from the transaction or experience ordinarily. One paragraph should be sufficient.

Results paragraph: What you expect them to do about it, the timescale you expect it to be completed within and the repercussions if they fail. Try to keep to one paragraph – or modify your demands.

Concluding paragraph: This is your parting shot. It can sting, it can be witty, but make sure it counts.

Yours sincerely (if you have used their name) OR Yours faithfully (if you have not)

Leave space here for your signature.

Your name (and job title if writing in an official capacity)
You can include your telephone number here if you choose.
And your email address here.

Chapter 8: Complaining for Fun

Complaints are essential if you have been wronged. Letter writing can be cathartic and a thoroughly enjoyable experience. Combining the two can be utter joy!

Complaining for fun and writing bizarre letters is nothing new. Over the years I have delighted in the correspondence of the satirist of William Donaldson, who published his letters as Henry Root (there's even a bistro inspired by him in London), Peter Cook's legendary and frequently bitter letters and Robin Cooper's *The Timewaster Letters*. All are worth looking through if you're seeking inspiration or want bite-sized chunks of entertainment to pass ten minutes alone in the smallest room.

When writing this book, I was introduced to a local man, Ahmed Dahl, who has been writing letters as a hobby for many years and I was stunned by the volumes of responses, gifts, signed photos and personal letters he has received from film and TV stars, sports personalities, politicians, religious leaders and businesses. What struck me most was that, despite many of Ahmed's letters causing eruptions of laughter, he writes them with the utmost seriousness and sincerity and not for a living but for his own pleasure of receiving post every morning. His filing system is meticulous, if a little too complicated for my liking, and the breadth of subjects, companies and individuals he has tackled is mightily impressive.

Because of Ahmed's reluctance to share his hobby and his lack of appreciation for other people's (potential) interest in his letters, he is completely unknown and only recently built a simple website, **www.ahmeddahl.com**, to make his letters available for others to enjoy. I don't think he's entirely happy that I found so many of his letters amusing but he allowed me to include a few here as an example of what can be achieved by complaining for fun.

Certainly much of what Ahmed writes has no relevance to your genuine complaints, but if I had the time and balls I'd be writing letters like his and, besides, this is *my* book and I like them enough to publish a few in it.

The following examples are a tiny selection of his correspondence to date but an inspiration to serious letter writers everywhere. If one unknown, unqualified, unemployed man who lives with his gran can achieve this, just think what you can do with good reason.

Ahmed Dahl

19 October 2006

Chief of Sending Food Out to Africa
ActionAid
Chataway House
Leach Road
Chard
Somerset
TA20 IFR

Dear Chief of Sending Food Out to Africa

I am concerned about the state of the world because some people are poor and starving to death and I think that it is wrong. What do you think? I can't believe that there is so much food in the world but it is not given to the people who are hungry but it is given to the people who have already eaten enough! This is wrong, and that is official.

I know this because my friend Bryan (David and Mark have not been abroad yet) came back from abroad and on the plane they gave him more food than he could eat and instead of wasting it he gave it to me but I think that there are other people in Africa and other countries like it that have had no food at all (!) and so they deserve it more than me because I am going to have my dinner later. I think it would be better if you sent it to them and so it won't be wasted on somebody (me) who will probably have enough. The extra food that they gave him is the cheese and ham baguette as you can see. I have also been kind enough to enclose 50p as a donation to help the cause. Please will you let me know who benefits from my kind donation as I would like to know that it is going somewhere good?

You might wonder why I am helping ActionAid and that is an easy question to answer. I discovered that you are in Chard and I have decided to help the town. I first heard about Chard when your school (Holyrood) had over a thousand students die on one day of a disease earlier this year. I wrote to the headmaster to tell him I was sorry for him but he has been too upset to reply.

Then I read about the Mayor of (you guessed it) Chard who fell in love with the Town Clerk by a map and got into trouble for it. Poor man. And then (would you believe it because I didn't I can tell you!) I read about ActionAid also being in Chard and I just knew that I had to help. Good things come in threesomes and it is probably a sign! You are very lucky that I am in tune with signs, I can tell you.

Anyway, good luck with finding food for everyone and please let me know how much good I have done today.

Yours sincerely

Ahmed Dahl.

117

fighting poverty together

3rd November 2006

Mr A Dahl

████████████████████

Dear Mr Dahl

Thank you very much for your recent letter. It was very kind of you to attempt to share surplus food with people who do not have sufficient, but I should advise you that this is not practical, just in case you are thinking of doing this again. The food had to be disposed of because it would not have been kept at an ambient temperature whilst travelling to us and it would not have been safe to eat. In addition I am sure you can appreciate the practicalities of transferring consumables with a limited shelf life overseas is difficult.

People make money donations to us and we transfer that money to the areas in greatest need and then whatever is needed is sourced locally. Donations such as yours go into our general fund and this money can be used in any of the countries where we work or to recruit new supporters or help our campaigning and advocacy work.

Thank you again for your kind thoughts and intentions. I am sending you a copy of our Common Cause magazine which you might like to share with your friends.

I have paid for the postage myself, Mr Dahl, as I would not like to take up the donation that you made to us with return postage, as of course there is always a cost involved in any communication and mailing.

With kind regards.

Yours sincerely

Dawn Wyatt
Development Team Manager
UK Supporter Services

ActionAid International UK is a unique partnership of people who are fighting for a better world - a world without poverty.

ActionAid International UK
Chataway House
Leach Road, Chard
Somerset TA20 1FR
United Kingdom

Telephone
++44 (0)1460 238 000

Facsimile
++44 (0)1460 67191

E-Mail
supporterservices@actionaid.org.uk

Website
www.actionaid.org.uk

International Secretariat
Johannesburg

Asia Region Office
Bangkok

Africa Region Office
Nairobi

Americas Region Office
Rio de Janeiro

Europe Region Office
Brussels

Founder
Cecil Jackson Cole

Executive Director
Richard Miller

Chair
Karen Brown

Patron
HRH The Prince of Wales

ActionAid is a registered charity No. 274467 Company registered Limited by guarantee Registered Office at the London address.

Ahmed Dahl

26 January 2006

The Right Honourable Alistair Darling MP
Department of Traffic and Roads
Labour Government Division
House of Commons
London
SW1A 0AA

Dear The Right Honourable Alistair Darling MP

On behalf of England I would like to thank you for dealing with all the White Van Men and giving them driving lessons. They are a hazard on the road and shouldn't be there. Also they are an eyesore as most of them are rusty and white shows up the rust more than dark blue.

As you probably know, I don't drive a white van and so I don't fit into your category but I think I could benefit from some more driving lessons to make me good. It doesn't seem fair that bad people get free gifts and good people (like me) don't. Why is that? The Conservatives gave free holidays to bad school children who beat their teachers up and I didn't ever beat my teacher up and nobody even thanked me for not doing it let alone gave me a free holiday and I could have done with one I can tell you! Why can't something nice be done for nice people (like me) who take the time to write to say how good people are (like you) instead of bitching behind their backs? I know it's not your fault but it isn't very fair.

There could be a rewards system for good people to collect points every week they don't do anything wrong. You could put it on the ID (Identity) card of you like and that way you'd definitely fool the Lords and Ladies into passing it. If you just go for, say, ten weeks without doing anything wrong, it counts as a good mark in case you accidentally speed or park in the wrong place later. If you collect fifty weeks you get a free cake and if you can do something like a thousand weeks you get the free holiday. I think you'll find people are much better behaved and crime levels are reduced. Please can we try it out? If I backdate it, I think I have probably collected about eighty nine weeks so far so please can you make a record of that on my file?

When you write back to me please may you send me a personalised autographed photograph (of you)? Thank you very much.

Yours sincerely

Ahmed Dahl.

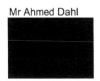

Department for
Transport

Khaleda Khatun
Sustainable Distribution Research Branch
Department for Transport
2/24 Great Minster House
76 Marsham Street
London
SW1P 4DR

Mr Ahmed Dahl

Direct line: 020 7944 2434
Fax: 020 7944 2928
Email: ██████████@dft.gsi.gov.uk

Web site: www.dft.gov.uk

22 February 2006

Dear Mr Dahl,

Thank you for your letter of 26 January 2006 to Alistair Darling, Secretary of State for Transport, concerning the training of van drivers. I have been asked to reply.

An explanation as to the background of SAFED and our vision of where it is going might help to allay your concerns that it rewards bad driving.

The Safe and Fuel Efficient Driving (SAFED) scheme has been highly successful in the truck sector. The Department undertook research in 2005 to study the van sector, to adapt and develop the existing scheme to be appropriate for vans and to pilot the training course to determine how effective it would be. The results were published on our website on 25 January 2006. A key stakeholder advisory group was formed to advise and steer this pilot project.

The new programmes takes the knowledge of better driving techniques developed through research, packages them into a one-day course and demonstrates the course on a substantial cohort of truck drivers. This will involve a significant number of instructors to ensure that the training could be continued on a commercial basis.

The scheme is to demonstrate the benefits of this type of training to persuade drivers and employers to embed it into normal practice, create market demand and fund it commercially. Instructors are trained to meet this market demand and offer the training service. With sufficient competing trainers selling SAFED training a true market should result and achieve good leverage of public funding.

I hope that this makes it a bit clearer and shows how this is a good scheme to help well intentioned people become better drivers creating a better environment for all.

Yours sincerely,

Khaleda Khatun

Ahmed Dahl

17 July 2009

Lord Sir Jeffery Archer, MP (Ret.)

Dear Jeffery Archer MP (Ret.)

Are you are okay or have you been ill for a long time? I hope not as you are a national institute. I am only concerned because I haven't heard anything about you recently and also you ignored my letters last year and the year before. I am not going to write to you again because four chances is enough and I have given you five. I will be very disappointed because Phil Collins has replied to as many letters as you have ignored and Tony and Cherry Bliar have replied to more and they are the enemy, so to speak. Do you know I have moved house because of Gran again?

The last thing I heard about you was your book about prison diaries and that was a long time ago. I would like to read it but I can't find it. Please may you send me an autographed copy that I can read? I enjoyed most of your books that I have read but I think that *Caine and Able* was the best so far. I don't think television did a very good film of it but at least the general public saw it. It is not good when your work is only appreciated by the literati (like you and me) as it deserves to be out there in the public domain. Do you have any new books on the way? I have some ideas if you would like to discuss them. I do not think I will ever have time to write a book as I am too busy with other things but it seems a shame to waste such good ideas and so I will happily give them to you if you would like them. Perhaps we can discuss it over coffee if you are in Bristol because I don't go to London much.

I am still very sorry that you did not make it to be Lord Mayor of London as you would have been far better than Ken Livingstone. Mind you, you were in good company as they wouldn't let Sir Richard Branson have it either. And the Powers That Be do not like Sir Richard Branson because he upset the Government's Airline Company (British Airways) and refused to have lunch with them and tried to buy Concorde and then wanted to run the National Lottery honestly, and I expect the Powers That Be just could not have that! So do not worry, you are in good company and respected by honest people (like me) even if you are not by the bad people in power. It is good that Boris Johnson has the job now though because at least he is on your side and you can always have another go when they let him back into the government.

At least you still have your main job as a writer to fall back on and haven't stooped to awful depths like George Galloway MP and been on *I'm a Celebrity Big Brother.* Do not do it! It will ruin your career and self-respect. Do you really want to be seen crawling around the floor licking people like a cat? I do not think so! Do you think that Chris de Burgh can put in a good word for you somewhere as you saved Kurdistan together and went to Miss World?

I do not wish to demean you, my Lord, but please would you send me a personalised autographed photograph when you write to me (with the book)? Thank you in advance.

Yours sincerely.

Ahmed Dahl.

JEFFREY ARCHER

Mr A Dahi

23rd July 2009

Dear Mr Dahi,

Many thanks for your letter of 17th July.

I'm afraid neither myself nor my PA recalls receiving any
earlier letters from you, but I appreciate you taking the
time to write and am happy to enclose a signed photograph
as requested.

It is kind of you to offer to share your story ideas with me, but
I already know the subjects of my next three books, so am not
looking for any new material at the present time.

With best wishes

Yours sincerely

Jeffrey Archer

www.jeffreyarcher.co.uk

To Armed Dahl,   Jeffrey Archer

Ahmed Dahl

5 February 2006

Manager of Chocolate Ingredients
Department of Chocolate Ingredients
Cadbury's Trebor Bassett
PO Box 12
Bourneville
Birmingham
B30 2LU

Dear Manager of Chocolate Ingredients

You must have almost the best job in the world. I love chocolate and English chocolate is the best in the world and that's official. It is good that you make it because Cadbury's has a good name that is respected and makes the best English chocolate. I particularly love your Flake, Dairy Milk, Yorkie Bar, and Bourneville dark plain chocolate. Is it a coincidence that you live in Bourneville or did you move there because of the chocolate? It's a bit like the haulage company called Chard and Axminster Transport that bought all the car number plates with CAT in them (like CAT 1 and CAT 2 and CAT 3 etc.) for their trucks. A really good and effective idea that reminds people of their name.

I heard on the news that you now have to print on the wrappers of your chocolate the entire ingredients so that people know which part is good for them and which part is bad for them and a government warning like on cigarette packets like **Eating Too Much Chocolate Makes You Fat If You Don't Get Exercise As Well** and **Chocolate Is Bad For Your Baby If They Don't Have Breast Milk And Vegetables Too.** I think that is a good idea to some degree as lots of people are ignorant and don't know that you have to eat vegetables and get exercise as well as chocolate but it will be a bad thing if the ingredients and government warning take up more space than the name. I hope this doesn't happen.

I used to like the Cabana bar when I was a boy but you don't make it any more and I wish you would. Please will you do it again? It was chocolate with soft biscuit base, coconut and chopped cherries and was your best chocolate apart from the Bourneville dark plain chocolate and Flake. Please will you do it again? Thank you very much.

I have entered some competitions on your Cadburys website but never won any chocolate or movie tickets which doesn't seem fair as I buy and eat so much of your chocolate. Please may you send me some as a special thank you for writing to let you know how great your chocolate is and for eating so much of it? Thank you very much again.

Keep up the good work and don't let the government's ridiculous new laws upset you. Nobody likes them anyway and they'll be gone soon (I hope)!

Yours sincerely

Ahmed Dahl.

PO BOX 12
BOURNVILLE
BIRMINGHAM B30 2LU
CONSUMER DIRECT LINE 0121-451 4444
SWITCHBOARD TELEPHONE 0121-458 2000
FAX No. 0121-451 4297
http://www.cadbury.co.uk

16 February 2006

Mr A Dahl

Our Ref:- 1237534B

Dear Mr Dahl,

Thank you for your letter which has been passed to me for response.

Please be assured that all comments do not go unheard and that the points you have raised in your letter have been passed to the Marketing Team and Regulatory Team for their information.

Because of the hundreds of requests for samples that we receive each year, it is our company policy not to send them out. Also, sending samples through the mail can sometimes mean that the product will arrive damaged and therefore would not be a good representation of our great chocolates.

I noted from your letter that you were enquiring about the history of the Company and so I am enclosing some Fact Cards which I hope you will find interesting.

Once again thank you for taking the time to contact us.

Yours sincerely

Sarah Welch
Consumer Relations Department

ENC. - FACT CARDS

Registered in England. Company No. 155256   Reg Office PO Box 12, Bournville, B'ham B30 2LU

Ahmed Dahl

23 February 2006

Mr Endemol
Endemol UK
Shepherds Studios
Charecroft Way
Shepherds Bush
London W14 0EE

Dear Mr Endemol

Firstly, I am very sorry that I haven't used your complete name but I'm afraid I don't know it. I asked my friends (David, Brian and Mark) and they all said this was your name and it would be okay if I didn't know your Christian or Moslem name as you would understand. I hope they are right and you do. Sorry if you don't.

I would like to be on *I'm a Celebrity Big Brother* if you have another series and I would like to let you know that I am available if the fee is right. I won't cause as much trouble as Pete Burns and will be more interesting than George Galloway.

You may not know much about me yet but you will do as I am going to be very famous one day soon when my show *Ahmed Dahl Versus the World* is picked up. Would you like to see a copy of the format? Maybe I could sell it to you as a joint deal – you buy *Ahmed Dahl Versus the World* and make it successful and I will become very famous and then help you out by being the star of your *I'm a Celebrity Big Brother* show. Shall we have a meeting soon to discuss it?

I know that you don't have an office in Dursley (as far as I know) but you do have one in Bristol and that is fairly close and so I can meet you there rather than you having to wait in London for me. Just get back to me and we'll arrange a date. Excellent!

In the meantime I have some other shows for you to think about too but I'll save those for when we meet. Thank you very much.

Yours sincerely,

Ahmed Dahl.

Brighter Pictures Ltd

Shepherds Building Central

Charecroft Way

Shepherds Bush

London, W14 0EE

Telephone 020 8222 4100

Facsimile 020 8222 4186

E-mail: info@brighter.co.uk

http://www.brighter.co.uk

20th March 2006

Mr Ahmed Dahl

Dear Mr Dahl

Thank you for sending us your idea.

As you may imagine, we are always developing our own ideas and formats and, when we are sent material by other people, it is often in the same area as projects we already have underway. I am afraid that Endemol UK does not, therefore, collaborate with outside creatives or accept unsolicited ideas from outside the company. This is partly to avoid any possible confusion as to the origin of our projects.

We normally suggest that you get in touch with a broadcaster and if they like your idea, they will suggest a meeting with a production company like us.

We wish you the best of luck for the future.

Kind regards,

Sharon Powers
CREATIVE DIRECTOR – BIG BROTHER

Part of Endemol UK plc

Registered office: Shepherds Building Central, Charecroft Way, Shepherds Bush, London W14 0EE Registered No 02697443 VAT No 466 5371 24

Ahmed Dahl

21 June 2006

The Right Honourable The Lord Mayor of Bristol,
Aka Councillor Peter Abraham
Lord Mayor's Office
The Mansion House,
Clifton Down,
Bristol, BS8 3LJ

Dear The Right Honourable The Lord Mayor of Bristol, Councillor Peter Abraham

As you remember I wrote to you last year (twice!) and as I remember you didn't reply (twice) and so I know that you won't reply to me this time either although hopefully one of your minions will again. I jolly well hope so as this is a very important and deeply worrying issue that needs to be addressed and you are the man to address it (with me) as you are the most important man in Bristol at the moment.

In short, BOMBS AWAY!!!

No, this isn't a war cry from the likes of Douglas Bader (God rest his soul as he is dead now) but it is a request that comes pretty close to a demand so to speak. My friend (Mark – you probably haven't heard of him as he hasn't written to you) told me that he was watching television the other day and that there was a news report telling him that Bristol has lots of WWII UXB (World War Two Unexploded Bombs) underground and in some buildings have been built on top of them. This is foolish and very worrying indeed especially if you live on top of a bomb which I don't because I live in Dursley and the Germans weren't interested in bombing Dursley because we didn't sell slaves or have docks. Mark said that there are either 793 WWII UXB or 297. He's not very sure because he was so shocked that he forgot to write down the exact number for me.

If it is the second number that is bad enough because it is enough to kill most of us. If it is the first number then that is even worse and disastrous! Just last week there was a bomb scare in Bristol when the WWII UXB turned out to be just a pipe or something. That was bad enough although it would have helped with the demolition of the buildings you are demolishing so that you can rebuild Bristol (well done – it needs it!).

What really worries me is that somebody on the television said that you know exactly where all of the WWII UXB are. That is very surprising as I cannot understand why you would leave them there if you know where they are. You do know that bombs kill people, don't you? Why would you put people's lives at risk? Was it somebody's job in WWII to list all the UXB? I wonder if it was a work experience person who didn't finish the job properly and then clear up the bombs they had listed. Even if that is the case you'd have thought (because I did!) that somebody else would finish the job. It has been 61 years since WWII finished and that is plenty of time to clear up the mess and not build shops and houses on top of the WWII UXB.

So what are you going to do about it, please? Is it still safe for me to visit Bristol or should I wait until the job is finished? Please may you also send me the personalised autographed photograph (of you) that you forgot to send me last time? Thank you very much indeed.

Yours sincerely

Ahmed Dahl.

Mr Ahmed Dahl

From	Mr D J Clark
Telephone	0117 903 1460
Fax	0117 903 1454
Our Ref	gen014
Date	4th July 2006

Dear Mr Dahl

I thank you for your letter addressed to the Lord Mayor dated the 21st June 2006. I am writing to advise you that the Lord Mayor is currently on annual leave and will not return until the 11th July when he will be shown your letter. As you are obviously worrying about the situation of unexploded bombs in Bristol I thought I should write as one of the Lord Mayor's "minions" as you called me, to alleviate some of your worries.

It is gratifying that someone who lives in Dursley is worried about the safety of the citizens of Bristol from unexploded bombs. As you are aware the local press reported that an incident involving a possible unexploded bomb had caused major problems in Bristol whilst the threat was checked out. As you are aware the threat turned out to be a false alarm. The press ran a story in which they gave the number of bombs which were dropped on Bristol and the number of those that did not explode. Both these figures were estimates as no-one knows how many bombs were dropped on Bristol or how many of those failed to explode. In the weeks and months following the bombing of Bristol, bomb disposal teams worked in the area, following up any leads and rendering unexploded bombs safe to ensure the citizens of Bristol were as safe as could be.

It is over 60 years since the bombing raids on Bristol and many years since any unexploded bomb has been found. The health and safety experts feel there is no significant threat to citizens from an unexploded bomb, however the plans are in place to ensure citizen's safety should an unexploded bomb be discovered. The disruption to the area around Broadmead was the result of those plans.

Please do not worry too much for our safety. Thank you for your concern in this matter.

Yours sincerely

D J Clark
Lord Mayor's Secretary

Central Support Services

Lord Mayor's Office
The Mansion House
Clifton Down
Bristol BS8 3LJ

Carew Reynell
Director of Central Support
Services

Website
www. bristol-city.gov.uk

Ahmed Dahl

11 October 2005

Louis Willem Gunning, President
Department of Marmite
Unilever Bestfoods UK
Crawley
RH10 3RQ

Dear President Gunning

Somebody is stealing our mail! I am sure that you replied to my letter of 27 August (this year) but the chances are somebody didn't want you to reply to me because they were jealous of my ideas and your response. Hopefully we can deal with them or at least sneak this letter (and your reply) past them.

But, to the main point: Thank you for coming to our great, but small, island to lead the world in food production with your idea for Marmite. I have to say that it is probably the greatest food invention of the past 450 years, although I must admit that I prefer chocolate.

I am confused by your advertising campaign, though. I can see why you want to make commercials for the people (like me) who love Marmite as we are already fans. I can also see why you would want to educate those people who are not sure. I have a friend who swore deaf and blind that she didn't like Marmite but I made her a sandwich with flora, cheese, mayo, tomatoes, lettuce, cucumber and, yes, you guessed it, Marmite. She said that she loved the sandwich and so I proved my point!

But getting back to my first point, I don't understand why you would want to advertise that people hate Marmite. Don't you think that it could be damaging? I did an experiment and told everybody at a dinner party recently that I hate coffee cake and told them all that they use pygmies to pick the coffee beans and lock them in a big tin shed and subject them to torture. When the lady brought out a coffee cake, nobody had any of it, so it goes to show how negative advertising can work against you.

I also don't understand why you have fans of Marmite being eaten by a big Marmite blob monster in your new commercial. Again, it is not good to make people who hate Marmite think that they are clever. I would suggest that you try a new angle in your next campaign. I have a few suggestions:

Husband and wife eating breakfast. Husband eats Marmite on toast but wife says he's sick as she hates it. They walk to work together and he has a warm Marmite glow to him and seems to be walking on small Marmite clouds under his feet. The wife falls down a manhole but he floats over it. Slogan: Hating Marmite will be the death of you!

Or: two campers walking through a forest. A bear comes after them and they run. One of them pulls out a jar of Marmite and offers it to his friend. The friend refuses it and says that it is disgusting. The first one shrugs, smears it on his hands and is able to climb a tree because it gives him extra adhesive abilities. The friend can't climb the tree and gets eaten by the bear. The last frame is the first camper up the tree licking his fingers and smiling. Slogan: Eat Marmite, don't get eaten.

I have plenty more ideas if you would like them as I want to help promote a great product.

Yours sincerely

Ahmed Dahl.

Marmite Consumer Care
Freepost NATE139
Milton Keynes
MK9 1BR

Freephone: 0800 136959
Minicom: 0800 0280173

Ref: 668855
Date: 20 October 2005

Mr A Dahl   668855

Dear Mr Dahl

We do appreciate you taking the time and trouble to write to us about your idea.

As an international company Unilever PLC and its operating companies receive many ideas so it is not possible to respond to proposals of this nature. We have numerous development teams who specifically research and explore ideas and they fully address our needs in this area.

We wish you every success with your idea but regret that we are unable to take advantage of your offer.

Yours sincerely

Hannah Lowrie
Consumer Care Advisor

Unilever

Unilever UK Foods
a trading name of Unilever Bestfoods UK Limited
Registered in England & Wales No. 43520
Registered Office: Brooke House, Manor Royal,
Crawley, West Sussex, RH10 9RQ

Ahmed Dahl

2 October 2005

Sir Richard George CVO, Chairman
Weetabix Ltd.
Burton Latimer
Kettering,
Northamptonshire
NN15 5JR

Dear Sir Richard George CVO

Congratulations on your Knighthood! You've probably had it for quite a while but I always think it is best to start a letter to a stranger with a compliment rather than launching straight to the point or into a complaint in case you put them off and they don't reply or even read the rest of the letter as they are upset. Hopefully I have avoided that, now.

I am greatly distressed as I remember eating Weetabix Weetaflakes when I was a young boy and I absolutely loved them but now you can't buy them any more. Please don't fob me off with the old boxes of Wheatflakes as they were completely different, much bigger and nowhere near as nice. Weetabix Weetaflakes were small flakes that looked similar to the individual flakes in a Weetabix but were much darker, not joined together in a Weetabix and sweeter. They also came in a big bag and not stacks in a box.

I have been looking for years but cannot find them and so can only assume that you have stopped making them. Please change your mind and make them again as they were absolutely my favourite cereal and I am *very* disappointed that I can't enjoy them any more. Feel free to rename them again (like the Mars Marathon/Snicker) if you have been taken over by the Americans just as long as they taste the same. Being English, I will see through that anyway, just as all of the English did with the Snickers débâcle.

Thank you and I shall look forward to hearing good news from you very soon.

Yours sincerely and in hope.

Ahmed Dahl.

Reference: 305-55-6/ajl/V3.00

October 6, 2005

WEETABIX LIMITED
WEETABIX MILLS
BURTON LATIMER
KETTERING
NORTHANTS NN15 5JR

T: 01536 721567
T: 01536 721566
F: 01536 724785
e-mail: consumerservice@weetabix.co.uk
web: www.weetabix.co.uk

Mr A Dahl

Dear Mr Dahl

Thank you for your letter of October 2.

In fact, Sir Richard George is no longer our chairman. He has taken on a non-executive director's role following the sale of the company.

The Weeta Flakes you remember (small, dark flakes packed in bags) were discontinued quite some years ago.

At present we have no plans to produce them again. However, if sufficient demand can be established we will of course reconsider the situation. Your enquiry will form part of our market research in this area.

We take all comments from our consumers seriously and always consider them in our attempts to provide the best possible breakfast cereals we can.

Once again, many thanks for taking the trouble to contact us. It was great to hear from you. Please accept the enclosed, sent with our compliments.

Yours sincerely

Dan Herrin
Consumer Services Man

THE QUEEN'S AWARDS
FOR ENTERPRISE
2004

Registered in England   Latimer, Northants   INVESTOR IN PEOPLE

Ahmed Dahl

2 July 2008

Colin Skellett, Executive Chairman
Wessex Water
Claverton Down
Bath
BA2 7WW

Dear Colin Skellett

I know we don't know each other but I know your name and face because it is on your website and so I hope you don't mind if I ask you some questions because I am being polite and not offensive.

First of all what is the difference between an Executive Chairman and a Normal Chairman, please? I know it sounds like a joke (like what is the difference between a duck? One leg is both the same. That's surrealism apparently but I still don't get it or find it funny because you have to have at least two things to have a difference between them and the answer is just very bad English so how can that be funny?) but it isn't because I don't know and would really like to. I expect you are better than a Normal Chairman but I don't understand why.

The other thing (second question) is why does my tea taste of bleach sometimes? I don't use bleach and we are not allowed it in the house with Gran after last time. I don't think it can be the teabags because it doesn't always taste like bleach just sometimes and we used to have PG Tips but now we have Yorkshire Gold. It can't be because we boil the water twice because we don't and I always empty the old water out for the kettle before putting new water in so to speak so that it doesn't make the element furry. What do you think it is please?

The other other thing is I've never seen you advertise on TV. Why don't you? Is it because you don't have anyone to write your adverts for you? I can do it for you if you like because I am very good and have a very good imagination. If you want a slogan you can start with 'Wessex Water doesn't taste of bleach and is good enough to drink!' or ' If Wessex Water is good enough for Ahmed Dahl and his Gran it's good enough for you!' Let me know what you think and how many more you want. I can do lots of them for you.

Thank you for the answers when they arrive.

Yours sincerely.

Ahmed Dahl.

EDWARD FIELD

Wessex Water

Claverton Down   Bath BA2 7WW   Telephone 01225 526000

Mr Ahmed Dahl

Direct line: 01225 526402
Direct fax: 01225 528009
Email: ███████@wessexwater.co.uk

7 July 2008

Dear Mr Dahl

Thank you for your letter of 2 July. The difference between an Executive Chairman and a normal Chairman is that an Executive Chairman is full time, whereas a normal Chairman is usually a part time non executive.

Your water is not supplied by Wessex Water but by Bristol Water so you need to contact them about the taste of the water.

Wessex Water does advertise on television and we currently have adverts running.

Colin Skellett
Chairman

Wessex Water

a YTL company

134

Chapter 9: Permission to Praise

In spite of all that has come before this, I don't complain very much. I have countless reasons to be grateful for each solitary occasion I have to complain. It is my firm belief that there is far more good in the world than bad; it's just that bad news often makes for a more exciting story if the newspapers and TV broadcasts are to be believed.

As I've stated repeatedly throughout this book, if the service or product is substandard, we should and must complain. It is our duty to do so, otherwise nothing will change, the scoundrels will continue to take our money, shortchange us and continue to not give a damn. We should rage against them, expose their ineptitude and lack of care and we should embarrass and humiliate them publically until they improve.

Equally, we have a responsibility to thank when the service is good and congratulate when it surpasses expectations.

When I was a child, we were en route to Cornwall for a rare family holiday and we stopped at a service station for lunch. The visit remains memorable for two reasons: Firstly, my father, an avid football supporter, spotted Howard Kendall, the

Everton manager at the time. I had no idea who he was (not until a couple of years later when Everton beat 'our' Watford in the FA Cup final) but I appreciated the awe and wondered if we should ask for his autograph. Dad dismissed my thought immediately. Mr. Kendall was also with his family and it wouldn't do to disturb him.

The second reason was the childish embarrassment I felt when my dad asked our waitress if he could speak with the manager. The manager duly arrived, apologised immediately for whatever his staff had done wrong and asked what it was that had upset Dad. Dad then also apologised, as all good Englishmen do, and explained that nothing was wrong but, on the contrary, the meal was superb and he wanted to express his gratitude to the manager and the chef. In hindsight, I'm guessing Dad didn't visit many service stations and he sure as hell didn't eat in fancy restaurants, but the look on the manager's face and his reaction made an indelible impression upon me. He was clearly taken aback and as he walked away, shoulders back and head held high, I heard him mutter in amazement "That's a first."

I recently received an email from the chairman of a company in response to mine. In it he wrote "...it is not often that people take the time to send bouquets – brickbats are more usual, although happily not too often! I really appreciate your note and will see that ███████ knows about it and gets recognition."

Saying a sincere "Thank you," costs nothing (okay, a stamp sometimes if you're going to be pedantic) but its value is inestimable. It is a very sad reflection of society that we find it easier to complain (or whinge silently behind backs) than to proclaim loudly "Thank you. You provide an excellent service, your customer care is wonderful and I am truly grateful to you and your staff."

When we complain, hopefully we receive a refund, possibly a gift and, ideally, the service improves next time around. I suspect, however, that though my complaints have been necessary and mostly successful, the recipient and those lower down the food chain who have been held responsible have subsequently not enjoyed their best day at the office. My guess is that when a chairman or CEO receives an email or letter of gratitude, his/her day lightens, the stresses of the job ease slightly and s/he passes it amongst colleagues and subordinates to celebrate and inspire them and to show that when they work to the best of their ability and go the extra mile or ten, it *is* appreciated. Imagine how *you* would feel if your CEO called you into the office and emailed a memo to the entire staff citing your achievements and congratulating you? Cloud nine? Walking on air?

If we show appreciation for every service, if we say thank you there and then, if we take a few minutes to phone, email or write to the organ grinders to say what went well, why it made our day and how grateful we are, it will surely inspire them and their staff to strive for perfection. There can't be many people who enjoy receiving complaints but even if some of us find compliments difficult to accept, who doesn't, deep down, like to know that other people think we are pretty splendid at what we do?

If your waiter/waitress knows that you appreciate him/her, that you tell the manager how wonderful s/he is and that you tip well, you can bet you'll receive more care and attention and great service every time you visit the restaurant in future. When staff know their work counts for something, they take more pride in it, they strive to maintain and exceed standards and that means a better experience for you and other customers. Everybody wins.

I have written *Permission to Rage* because I'm cheesed off with poor service, with companies that suck and don't care enough to change. My complaints work for me and I hope they make a difference in the long run for you, too. Complimentary letters and expressions of gratitude, on the other hand, *always* have a positive result that benefits everyone.

For the cynical few sitting at the back and muttering about not having time or it being a foolish attitude, sometimes writing thank you letters brings an immediate and personal reward, too. It isn't why I say thank you and I don't generally receive a response to my thank you letters – I express my gratitude because it is right to do so – but sometimes a bonus lands on my doorstep.

Last year I wrote to Taylors of Harrogate. Their Yorkshire Gold tea is my brew of choice and I always cut out the tokens from the boxes of tea. It used to be that one could exchange the tokens for tea towels, aprons, mugs, toy vans and cakes etc. but they changed the scheme so that tokens are now exchanged for a donation to their Yorkshire Rainforest Project. It is a worthy cause and I don't need any more mugs so I wrote to them with my latest batch of tokens, congratulated them on the change and asked them where else I could buy their cakes, now that I couldn't exchange tokens for them. A week or so later, I received a fab letter thanking me for mine and for my support of the new rainforest scheme. They informed me of a local stockiest of their cakes (no more, alas, if anybody at Taylors is reading this) and enclosed a voucher to enjoy one on them. It was unexpected, unnecessary and a complete joy to receive.

It isn't a recent lesson, either. My parents instilled in me an appreciation for others and a compulsion to show an interest and express my gratitude for even the most mundane of tasks. As a child, I used to chat to the cooks at school, holding up the queue, and ask about the food they had cooked. At both my junior and senior school the cooks soon learned my name and my passion for cake and periodically I would discover that they had set aside a larger portion or something particularly special for me. When I asked one of the cooks for the recipe for her jam macaroon and expressed my dismay that the dessert wasn't available more often, the following day she handed me a sheet of paper with my request with one hand and a plate with a double portion of macaroon with the other. I reckon I made her day, she certainly made mine, macaroon appeared on the menu with greater frequency and I'd like to think she and her colleagues enjoyed their work a little more even if a certain child did talk incessantly to them.

And so to my customer care heroes...

Top ~~Ten~~ Five Heroes (in my experience)

I really wanted to have a top ten to balance my list of scoundrels from Chapter 7 but, despite my efforts and requests to numerous friends, five was all I could come up with. What a sorry state! Hopefully there will be better news and an expanded list in the second edition of *Permission to Rage*. For now, though, allow me to celebrate with you the outstanding companies in my experience when it comes to after-sales care, customer consideration, problem solving and all-round brilliance.

1. **Apple (Cabot Circus, Bristol)** – I have never had cause to complain. If I have a problem, I take my MacBook or iPhone in and they take care of it, almost always without charge. The team members are knowledgeable, friendly and always willing to help and advise.

Quality Control: **10/10** Customer service and after sales care are second to none. Why would I buy a computer anywhere else?

2. **Halfords** – See **Case Studies 2** and **14** (pages 23 & 141) for details. Yes, it went badly wrong, but they did everything within their power to put it right even when I just wanted to walk away.

Quality Control: **10/10** Guess where I'm going to buy my wife's bike?

3. **British Telecom Broadband** – We had an awful time with them as **Case Study 13**, below, attests, but…

Case Study 13 – BT Broadband

This was a painful experience from the outset. The letter tells you all you need to know.

Squircle Entertainment

Not quite a square; not quite a circle...

edward@squircleentertainment.com   www.squircleentertainment.com
Squircle Entertainment,
+44 (0)   Twitter: @edwardsquircle

18 March 2012

Ian Livingston, CEO
British Telecom
81, Newgate Street
London
EC1A 7AJ

Ian   .com

Dear Mr. Livingston

Reference Account: GB

I think it is only fair to inform you that I shall not be paying my BT bill this month. Next month I may pay £2.00 and I shall consider what I pay the following month. I look forward to you taking me to court because I will not pay any fines or costs and will very publically go to jail as a matter of principal. I look forward to the publicity that the court case will bring both you and me, as I become the first member of the public to be jailed because BT refused to fulfil its obligations.

At this juncture I think it's important to point out that I do not have a criminal record. I have never been arrested or even questioned by the police. I have three points on my licence for exceeding the national speed limit and once received a detention at secondary school some twenty-five years ago. I'm guessing I'm not high on the list of wanted criminals.

In September, my wife (her criminal activities are fewer than mine) and I moved to our current address and entered into a simple contract with BT: You supply our telephone line rental and broadband with a minimum of 4GB and I pay my bills in full and on time. You will see from my account that I have unwaveringly upheld my side of the contract, paying in full every single month by direct debit.

Our telephone service is intermittent. Whist we don't use it often, the occasional interference on the line makes conversations impossible. It is a poor service but we can live with it because it isn't constant and we have mobile phones. The broadband service, however, is diabolical. On a reasonably good day, we have a download speed of 0.125GB and an upload speed of 0.344GB. I think you'll agree that is below the promised minimum of 4GB. Frequently, four times today for example, the broadband cuts out completely. Sometimes we lose our service for days at a time. Sometimes it is just for an hour or two several times a day. Occasionally we manage to go for a fortnight without it cutting out at all and just contend with the very slow speeds.

I have complained to BT on numerous occasions and several tests have been run on our line. Apparently there is nothing wrong with the line. Apparently our service is fine. Apparently we are not important enough to warrant return calls, confirmation of the progress, status reports, apologies, solutions or offers of a compromise and reimbursement. The several individuals I spoke with on my most recent call on 29th February 2012 asked me exactly the same questions and had evidently not conversed with each other or understood the situation at all. At the fourth request to describe the junction box and the fourth cause to bite my tongue as I explained *yet again* what the issue was, I still managed to refrain from screaming at your staff and was polite, albeit clipped, in my conversation.

The reward made it all worthwhile: Nobody made the promised phone call to inform me of the situation, my junction box is still open, the modem is still connected to the engineer's socket inside because nobody has called me back, as promised, to say the situation has been resolved and I can reassemble the box and, after a week and a half of standard, poor service, we have reverted to non-existent service for periods of the day.

Following the numerous, repeated conversations on the 29th, I received another phone call from a member of your staff asking me for feedback despite my opting out of the survey at the start of my calls. An hour later another member of your staff phoned me and asked me to increase my commitment to BT by agreeing to let your inept company supply us with your television service. Through gritted teeth I politely declined.

Based on the experience of our six-month contract to date, I believe BT is run by, at best, inept staff who hope that I will give up and accept the appalling service in return for their sycophantic attitude, insincere apologies and empty promises and, at worst, by corrupt individuals who want my money and my silence and don't give a damn.

I'd welcome your verdict and interpretation of the situation.

If BT had the balls to admit that it, as a company, and they, as individuals, have an unresolvable problem, apologised and offered us a reduction of 75% on our monthly bills, a rather generous proposition on my behalf bearing in mind we are receiving substantially *less* than 75% of the service promised, then I would accept it, deal with the frequent problems but accept that I was receiving the service I pay for. But to continue in this vein and persist with charging us the full rate is akin to selling me a brand new car and expecting me to be content when three of the wheels fail to rotate on a regular basis.

So, to reiterate, I am not going to pay BT this month and I will decide what to pay you in future months depending on the service you provide. I shall send this letter to you via email and post and await your response. Naturally I would prefer not to be fobbed off with a standard letter from one of your minions that does not address the situation although I fully expect to be completely ignored in line with what I assume is your current policy.

And I shall sit here and wait to be arrested and charged so that I may explain to all who care to listen exactly how BT and you, Mr. Livingston, treat your customers.

Naturally, I shall report you to OFCOM and will write to my local MP, Jacob Rees-Mogg, to warn him of my need of his assistance in raising the matter in the House of Commons. I shall also contact the national tabloids and broadsheets as I will require publicity and financial support. I'm sure you will understand my need as I am an individual in a tiny village and you head a multi-billion pound company. I'm feeling magnanimous and so I shall give you seven days before I write the other letters, copies of which I shall send you for your reference.

I look forward to your swift response.

Yours sincerely

Edward Field.

Success rating: 8/10 – I shouldn't have needed to escalate it to this level, but once I reached the Chairman, one of their 'top' engineers was put on it, he discovered the fault was with the box on the telegraph pole in our road. The box was replaced, we received a full refund on ALL bills paid to date and were given a further three months free of charge as an apology.

Quality Control: **8/10** It took a while but we got there. BT made amends, apologised profusely refunding all bills and giving further compensation. Since that situation, in the past few months, we encountered problems once again and they sent us a new modem that day without charge and the problem was again resolved. That said, there is still the ongoing 'Honourable Mention' issue...

4. **Cineworld Cinemas** – What? After all the grief I've had, why is Cineworld on my list of heroes? One word: Scott.

Quality Control: **8/10** Shortly before publication of this book, the issues with my Unlimited card arose yet again. After two emails and a phone call I reached a new customer service manager, Scott, who kept his promises, returned all my calls, emailed regularly, resolved the long-running and tedious issues with my account and credited one month's payment. He was calm, polite, professional and double-checked everything to ensure the problem was resolved permanently. More than that, he gave every impression of genuinely caring about rectifying the situation. It's a great pity that Scott doesn't wield more power within Cineworld, but I'm grateful for the small amount of influence he *does* have. And, yes, I did write both to Scott and the chairman, Tony Bloom, to express my gratitude. Credit where credit is due. Always!

5. **Taylors of Harrogate** – See the paragraph on page 137. A fine company that produces great tea and some very fine cakes.

Quality Control: **10/10** I have had no reason to complain to Taylors of Harrogate at all and my one letter of thanks and enquiry was responded to with a great letter and a coupon for a free cake. It doesn't get much better than that!

I recall several years ago one of the highest profile TV newscasters expressing a desire to end every evening news programme with a positive story to counter the doom and gloom that comprises a good 95% of our daily news. He was dismissed, mocked and humiliated for his opinion by his peers and certain quarters of the public and the idea didn't last long. Personally I think it was a noble effort to focus on the good and I applauded his endeavor. After 95% (give or take) of bad news in this book, I'm going to give you my final case study in honour of him. It is my greatest cause to celebrate in my long history of complaining. Ladies and gentlemen, Halfords.

Case Study 14 – Halfords

As **Case Study** 2 shows very clearly, this was a terrible experience that had 'doom' written all over it. I wanted to walk away but, contrary to all my expectations, Halfords as a whole, and three individuals in particular, turned the situation around spectacularly. Consequently, I remain a loyal customer and when I buy accessories or finally upgrade my bike in a few years, it will be Halfords that I visit. Their generosity and spectacular customer care cost them in the short term, but I have recounted this story to numerous people and I'd like to think that Halfords has been justly rewarded with sales and other loyal customers as a result.

Squircle Entertainment

Not quite a square; not quite a circle...

edward@squircleentertainment.com   www.squircleentertainment.com   www.squiss.co.uk

Squircle Entertainment,

+44 (0)   Twitter: @edwardsquircle

8 July 2014

███████, EA to the Chairman
Halfords Group plc
Icknield Street Drive
Washford West
Redditch
Worcestershire
B98 0DE

███████@halfords.co.uk

Dear Ms. ████

I am afraid I don't have John ██████'s email address, so please would you be kind enough to forward a copy of this letter to him today and ensure that Matt and Ben at your Eastgate store also read this?

Yesterday afternoon John phoned me and we spoke at length about the situation. He was very apologetic both for the problems with the bike and also his oversight in phoning me. He stressed again his, and Halfords', desire to rectify the situation with a replacement or refund although he pressed the point that he and the team would prefer to make amends rather than see me walk away. He asked me to think about it overnight and promised to call me this morning to chat further.

At just before 10.00 this morning, as promised, he telephoned me again and listened to my reasoning. Whilst I was very appreciative of his offer of an upgraded replacement I felt not anger but an overriding sense of dismay and disappointment and repeated that that I would prefer just a refund and to then walk away from the situation. He expressed how sorry he was to hear that but acquiesced and promised to phone Matt, the manager at your Eastgate store, and then call me straight back to confirm that Matt and/or Ben would be waiting for me at midday to arrange the refund. We ended the call pleasantly but, I think, with both of us feeling disappointed.

I arrived at the shop at midday with the sole desire and intention of handing over the bike, receiving the refund and departing within five minutes, unlikely ever to return again. Ben, however spent some time chatting with me while Matt was with another customer. He said that Matt was hoping to give me an upgraded bike as well as a refund but, again, I was dismissive; I didn't require anything that wasn't mine and that I didn't deserve but wanted to leave as soon as possible.

As soon as Matt was free, he again apologised profusely, reiterated all that John had said and explained that they had already built a Carrera Crossfire for me to have, whether I wished to keep it or sell it. I was initially reluctant but Matt was gently persuasive and he and another gentleman, whose name escapes me, who had built the bike talked about the attributes of the Carrera. Matt spent almost an hour with me, all told, and when I relented and agreed to accept the bike, he insisted that I accept the refund as well, even though I was content with the replacement bicycle.

I cycled around the car park a couple of times and the experience in just that short time was all that I had originally hoped for; it rides beautifully and the gear changing was smooth and effortless. I am looking forward to taking it out properly this evening and putting it to the test on the hills around me.

Even after the time and care that John had taken, I felt low and disappointed and wanted nothing more from Halfords. However, such was the care, attention and thoughtfulness that, contrary to all that I previously felt, I am overwhelmed by the desire and effort of Halfords as a whole and John, Matt and Ben specifically to not merely rectify a poor experience but to turn it around so completely.

Just as I feel it is my right to complain when things go awry, I feel it is my responsibility and, in this case, my pleasure to thank and congratulate you, Halfords and your staff for the exemplary way they have acted to ensure that I departed an incredibly, and unexpectedly, satisfied customer. I shall certainly return and, further to my discussion with Matt, shall look forward to a relationship with Eastgate store and one day buying my next bike from them.

If you would like me to write a reference or if you need me to write to anyone else to confirm this, please feel free to contact me.

Thank you and best wishes.

Yours sincerely,

Edward Field.

The negative issues have filled most of this book but I would like to end here on a positive note. Patient Reader, thank you for buying this book and reading my rant. All the way through this book I have given you permission to rage.

Now, I give you permission to praise!

Disclaimer

The advice and suggestions in this book are based on my own experiences and successes. I have had no legal training at all, am not qualified in the eyes of the law to advise you and I am not responsible for any actions you take or for the consequences of your actions.

Take responsibility for yourself. Learn from me by all means, but be a big boy/girl and stand on your own two feet. Don't bother trying to sue me; I'm a penniless writer. And besides, I can run much faster than you.

Happy complaining.

Edward Field aka The Squiss
October 2014

About the Author

Edward lives.

He also eats cakes, feeds the mice and birds, and regularly watches a sparrowhawk eat the mice and birds in his garden.

Edward trained as a stage manager and now works mostly in the dark world of corporate events as a venue producer, scriptwriter and VOG, while his written work graces documentary sleeves, other people's books, websites for motorhomes and weddings and three textbooks on the South African curriculum.

He is the winner of the Golden Nail Award and the Dennis Cartledge Award, although neither has very much to do with writing.

There is more, and he is happily searching for it.

Edward publishes film reviews, fiction, inspiration, rants and cake recipes at **www.squiss.co.uk**

Printed in Great Britain
by Amazon